If you have any doubt about the continuation of Life after the death of the physical body, read this book. The author masterfully applies the scientific method to the many forms of evidence that support the continuation of Life, including Near-Death Experience, Deathbed Visions, Reincarnation, and After-Death Communication. These experiences are drawn from people of all religions, cultural groups, atheists, and historical times. Dr Parisetti evaluates each mode of experience for the quality of its evidence, asks and answers the skeptic's questions, and demonstrates how the "collective weight" of all these sources of evidence reveals an astounding "yes" to Life after Life.

Betty J. Kovacs, PhD
The Miracle of Death: There Is Nothing But Life
Merchants of Light: The Consciousness That Is Changing The World

Step into the Light

Transform your fear of death
by learning about life after life

Piero Calvi-Parisetti, MD

OpenMind

Openmind Publishing – March 2021

ISBN: **9798724735209**

© Piero Calvi-Parisetti

Contacts:

- drparisetti.com
- pcalvip@gmail.com
- facebook.com/stepintothelightbook

Contents

	An important introduction	1
1	What is it that really dies at death?	9
2	Unhelpful beliefs on death and the afterlife	15
3	Bases for a rational belief in life after life	19
4	What are Near-Death Experiences and why is it reasonable to trust them?	31
5	What deathbed visions are, and why we should trust them	63
6	Who are spirit communicators, and why is it reasonable to trust them?	83
7	Before we die	111
8	The moment of death	125
9	The early afterlife	137
10	The life review	147
11	The illusion of summerland	155
12	The first heaven	167
13	Stepping into the Light	185
14	Reincarnation	203
	Important conclusion	217
	Appendix A – Sources and essential bibliography	223

An important introduction

This is the fifth book I have written on the subject of what I like to call the *unbelievable truth* and, in many ways, it's a different kind of book. First, I have to admit that, given my education and professional background, so far I have been writing mostly for "left brain" people – people with an interest in (if not knowledge of) science and with a natural disposition for rational thinking. To some extent, I also wrote to try to convince the sceptics (tough luck there!), or at least those who have doubts and are amenable to being convinced by facts. Secondly, I have been writing mostly with the bereaved in mind. Early on in my studies and research, I realised that what I was learning about life after life could be of great help to those in pain because of the loss of a loved one.

However, there is another, pretty large group of people for whom learning about the *unbelievable truth* can have powerful, transformative beneficial effects. These are the people who are afraid of death, their own or that of a loved one. There are also those who may not be outright afraid, but simply nervous, uncertain, wanting to know what happens when we die, if anything at all. If you recognise yourself in these broad categories, this fifth book of mine is especially directed at you.

As you read on, please remember that I am a Western-educated medical doctor and long-time university lecturer. I am, or at least was, the intellectual product of a system that maintains that everything and anything that exists is physical matter – if you cannot touch it, measure it, it simply does not exist. What we call the mind is nothing other than the activity of our physical brain. When the brain stops functioning, at the moment of what we call death, the mind goes with it. Lights off, pure and simple.

For many years I had taken this worldview for granted, but now I understand that I was not thinking critically. Like many others in the scientific and medical fields, I was just accepting a worldview, a set of ideas, a theory that has almost become dogma in our society.

This will help you understand why the *truth* I write about indeed looked *unbelievable* to me for a long time.

However, the same scientific background that proved a hindrance in one way was of great help in another. Science, in fact, is not a fixed set of ideas or theories. Science is a *method*. It is a very effective way to learn about, understand and explain the world. And the method is very simple – it has only one fundamental instruction: *follow the evidence*. Look at the *facts*. Look at *what happens*, and on that basis alone build theories and provide explanations.

So, it was by *following the evidence,* in a scholarly research work that has lasted now for nearly 20 years, that I had to finally conclude that, as unbelievable as it may seem, the *truth* is indeed the truth.

Put in its simplest form, the truth is that *we do not die.* Our bodies stop functioning, the activity of our brains ceases, but "we" go on living. Anybody who has looked at the colossal mass of evidence with the care and attention it deserves, and is intellectually honest, can only draw one conclusion: in a way which we do not understand, what we consider to be "us" – our mind, our personality, our memories, our perceptions, our affections – does not cease to exist when the physical body stops functioning. What we call death is not the end of life. Rather, it is a passage, a transition into a new dimension of existence. Dying means stepping into a bright, luminous, fascinating dimension which is not physical, not material, but appears to us "more real than physical reality", as many have told us. In fact, many have simply called it *the light.*

So, coming to the purpose of this book, I will talk to your reason with the aim of trying to reach your heart. The reason to do that is simple, and is best explained by referring to a very interesting study carried out by Dr Kenneth Ring, one of the foremost researchers on the phenomenon we call Near-Death Experiences (in short, NDEs). Later in the book you will find an entire chapter dedicated to this baffling and wondrous phenomenon, so I won't go into any explanation here.

What you need to know now is that plenty of studies show a number of beneficial psychological and behavioural changes in those who've had such an experience. In short, one may say that people who have an NDE come back as better persons: they become less interested in material things and more interested in knowledge for its own sake; they move towards an all-embracing, compassionate form of spirituality, leaving behind any rigid religious dogma; they become more generous, caring, giving. And, most importantly, their fear of death is erased, completely and forever. These people are sure that there is life after life because they are convinced that *they've been there*. They had a direct, first-person experience of the afterlife, an experience which they invariably describe, as I said before, as "more real than reality".

A very interesting finding from Dr Ring's research is that these beneficial changes show up not only in those who actually had the experience, but also in people who only *read* about NDEs – the more they read, research and study, the more pervasive are the changes.

This effectively demonstrates that *knowing* about the evidence for life after life *can* transform the fear of death. The fact that such knowledge can considerably ease the pain of the bereaved is well known, to the point of being employed in certain grief counselling methodologies. I am convinced that the same knowledge can be of great help to those who, for whatever reason, are in fear of death.

If you belong to this category, please read with attention the following statements.

Your mind, your personality, your consciousness, your memories, all that you identify with yourself, with your feeling of being alive, are not dependent on your functioning physical brain.

When your brain dies, your mind and personality will continue to exist. It will still be you, and it will feel exactly like you, only without a physical body.

You most probably have gone through this transition from the physical to the spiritual world many times already, as this is not likely to be your first incarnation.

After the demise of your physical body, you will spend a certain amount of time in the various levels of the spirit world, and then you will probably, but not necessarily, incarnate again.

In the long term, all this pans out as a project for your own evolution and development. Life, in the material and spiritual worlds, has meaning and purpose.

Now, imagine that you were fully convinced that these statements reflect reality. Not convinced simply because you *want to believe*, but convinced because you trust the sources of this knowledge. You have looked into who is providing this information, you have critically examined the evidence, considered possible alternative explanations, and rationally come to the only possible explanation: that the sources of this information are indeed who they claim they are. I am talking about people who have temporarily crossed the threshold between the earthly, material world and the spiritual, nonmaterial world (as in the case of Near-Death Experiences and Deathbed Visions), and discarnate personalities who once walked the earth and now communicate with us through gifted mediums and various other channels. Imagine for a moment that your *reason* was convinced. How would your *heart* feel?

So, *this* is the purpose of my book. After a couple of initial chapters clearing the way from some common misconceptions, and after a broad, general overview of what we consider to be evidence, you will find three major, substantive chapters. In those, we will engage in a sort of scientific detective work, essentially aimed at establishing the credibility of our sources of information on the process of death and what comes afterwards. We will look at empirical evidence – that is *facts,* what happens – and we will see that evidence points without a doubt to the survival of personality to bodily death. Since this is a preposterous conclusion, we don't want to take it at face value. We will discuss and dissect a number of possible alternative explanations which have been proposed by critics, and we will see that not one of them is capable of accounting for the facts. I hope I will be able to show that, as I said earlier, the only possible explanation is that these sources are indeed what or who they claim to be, and therefore it is reasonable to trust them.

We will then proceed to describe the process of dying and what happens when we have shed our material body, based on the coherent, consistent testimony we received from these different sources.

Please understand that, although this is neither an academic nor a scholarly book, what you are embarking on is not necessarily a walk in the park. You will have to absorb masses of information which may be entirely new to you. Some of this information is relatively complex - sometimes scientific in nature – and will require your full attention and concentration. Other pieces of information may challenge some of your existing beliefs, or perhaps even your "capacity to believe", as the empirical evidence we'll be discussing can at times really be stranger than fiction. I strongly encourage to work through this large amount of information with the care it deserves.

This effort on your part will be rewarded in two very important manners. On the one hand, you will likely see your fear of death, or any concerns you may have about the process of dying and what comes afterward, completely transformed. On the other, you will definitely improve your experience of the afterlife, especially during what we will describe as the initial stages. This is an important subject, one that we will discuss at some length later in the book. The bottom line is that we are consistently told by our sources that the more we know what to expect, the easier the transition is from material to nonmaterial existence. Therefore, you will want to learn and to reflect on what you have learnt, for any effort you make today will improve your life tomorrow, on both ends of the threshold. In this respect, summing up a lifetime of study and research, Swedish-American psychiatrist and psychical researcher Carl Wickland concluded:

> "[My research] has proven conclusively that death is only a sleep and an awakening, the process of awakening depending largely upon the individual's mental attitude, such as religious bias, unreasoning scepticism, or the wilful ignorance of and indifference to life's meaning, so prevalent among the multitude."

Finally, as a way of ending this introduction, I would like to share with you a simple sentence that encapsulates all that I have come to believe after nearly 20 years of scholarly study in the field of psychical research. Please, take it to heart – meditate on it, profoundly, and often. This is not wishful thinking or an article of faith - it's the rational conclusion of a man of science. It can also be your first, fundamental step in transforming the fear of death.

We are not a body, with a consciousness we lose at death.

We are consciousness, with a body we lose at death.

Chapter one

What is it that really dies at death?

If I were to say to you "Show me yourself," you would probably say "What are you talking about?" And if I insisted, and asked you to show me, to point to something that you identify with yourself, you would probably do what everybody else does – point a finger to somewhere in the middle of your chest and say "That's it, this is me."

What you're pointing to is your body, this reassuring, solid body that's been with you for so many years. Yes, there's been growth, and changes, and ageing, but fundamentally your body feels the same from one day to another, from one year to another. With your finger pointing at yourself you feel the familiar texture of the underlying bone, and what appears more solid in our body than bone? Bone is like stone, right? And stone doesn't change. Stone is probably the closest thing to eternal we can think of. And, if you tap with your finger onto your sternum, that feels exactly like a stone. You are convinced that all the bones that support your body have been with you forever. Once you had grown up, that was it - these were your bones, your skeleton, and this is what you are touching now. This is the same bone you had yesterday, and last year. That's "you". Or is it?

No, it is not. Bone constantly turns over as part of what is called the *remodelling* process. Specialized cells called osteoclasts continuously re-absorb bone and at the same time other cells called osteoblasts form new bone. In the adult, about 10% of the entire bone mass is turned over each and every year. One tenth of the material that made up your sternum a year ago has gone, and has been replaced by new material. This is definitely not the same object you would have touched a year ago.

Do you think that's fast? Think again. Most other tissues in the human body change at a much faster pace. The need to replace old cells with new ones is different depending on the particular function of the tissue or organ, and so speeds vary. Certain white blood cells, for instance, live only a couple of hours.

Do you think that's fast? Think again. If you get inside the cells that make up your body, you see molecular processes unfolding at breath-taking speed. Just think of breathing, for instance. Think of the never-ending process of exchanging carbon dioxide for oxygen in the lungs: trillions of molecules of haemoglobin changing status every second. All those red blood cells entering the lungs full of carbon dioxide are most definitely not the same objects when they leave, full of oxygen.

Two thirds of your body – I mean two thirds of what you're showing me as "you" – is actually water. Do you want to tell me that that is the same water from this morning, yesterday, last week, or last year? Think for a moment of how much water you have drunk during the last twelve months, and how much you have lost. I can tell you – it's not far from a thousand litres. A ton of water – ten to fifteen times your body weight.

And I could go on with food. All the tons of food you have consumed in your life. All these external substances that you have assimilated. They have "become you". And all the tons of materials you have eliminated through digestion. They "were you", if you stick to the idea that you are your body, and where are they now?

I could go on and on with other examples, but I think you're getting my point now. Our identifying ourselves with our bodies is fundamentally wrong, because our bodies are not fixed, defined entities. Our bodies are better defined as enormously dynamic, open systems: they are in continuous transformation, and continuously exchange matter and energy with the environment.

Your body now is definitely not the same thing it was a second ago, or yesterday, or a year ago.

And still, we all have the overwhelming intuitive feeling that there is such a thing as a material "ourself" – a sense of continuum, of permanence, of unity with our flesh and bones. I will come back to that in a moment. First, I would still like to tackle the body issue from another angle.

Talking about cells, molecules and metabolism, we have taken the path of science. The mistaken perception we have about our body, however, can also be shown by logic. This is the path taken, for instance, by Buddhism, which teaches, amongst other things, about the impermanence of anything material. In fact, Buddhist masters go even further. They demonstrate through logic that there isn't even such a thing as an independently existing body. The reasoning of the masters is quite sophisticated – I will try to make it very simple with one example.

Take hold of your left hand with your right one, and ask yourself "What am I touching?" You may answer "I'm touching my body, I'm touching myself." But think again. What are you really touching? It's your hand, which is not your body. A part of it, but not your body. And think even further. What are you really touching? It's the skin covering your hand, which is not your hand. It's a part of it, but not your hand. And we could go on with the layers of the skin, and then the surface cells, and then the atoms, etc. The bottom line is that you cannot take a part and call it the whole. A "body" does not exist independently from its parts, but none of the parts can be called the body. You cannot point to something and tell me "That's my body". Our perception of material objects, including our body, as independently existing things is just an illusion.

If the perception of our bodies as independently existing, never-changing objects is an illusion, why then is this illusion so strong? Why are you, like anybody else, intuitively convinced that you are your body, that you as your body exist independently of anything, and that that body is basically the same throughout a lifetime? I think the answer lies in evolution. Our primary goal as biological systems in life is to survive. The fight for survival leaves little space for philosophising, and even less space for a perception of oneself that is less than solid, material, permanent. So, all these arguments are pushed away, or never really considered, and we get on with our good old body.

This useful illusion has served you well during your life so far, but right now is giving you big, big problems. You may have seen your body changing fast, perhaps because of a disease. You are afraid that at a certain point this highly dynamic system we call the body will cease to function. Your body will die. And since you are convinced that you are your body, you will die with it.

But we have shown that there is no such thing as an independently existing, unchanging body, and that our identifying ourselves with it is an illusion. This is further confirmed by observing a corpse: one hour, or one day after a person's death the body still exists. The flesh and bones are still there. From the biological point of view, a dead body is as teeming with life, changes, chemical reactions as a live one. You can still indulge in the illusion, and point to the body as an independently existing object. If the person was the body, and the body still exists, then the person should still exist. But no, you know the body is dead, and you are convinced that the person doesn't exist anymore. And you fear that this is what is going to happen to you.

If we are not our body, what is it then that makes us feel alive, and that we fear losing? What is it, really, that gives us this sense of continuity, unity, permanence from one day to another, from a year to another, throughout an entire lifetime? What is it that it is really unchanging, that we can truly call ourselves?

It's our consciousness. Our personality, our thoughts, our memories, our awareness, our sensations. That is what makes us feel alive, and that is what we really fear may come to an end with the death of our bodies, and in particular of our brain.

An even stronger, persistent illusion, fuelled by our intuition and from the misunderstanding of certain findings of science, is that our consciousness is located in and dependent on the brain. What we call death is essentially the end of the stupendously complex activity of the brain. When your EEG is flat, when there is no electrical activity in the brain, you are pronounced dead, and you as a person won't exist anymore.

As we will see shortly, impressive amounts of evidence indicate otherwise.

Chapter two
Unhelpful beliefs on death and the afterlife

Ever since I have been studying the evidence for survival of human personality after physical death, the question of religious beliefs has been nagging at me. This has turned into outright discomfort since I have moved into the field of counselling for the bereaved and the dying.

It is difficult for me to approach this subject, because the last thing I want to do is to come across as disrespectful for what are likely to be the most cherished, fundamental beliefs for so many people around the world. I insist in saying that, although I am not religious myself, I do fundamentally respect religions and religious people.

Nevertheless, I cannot help but noticing that many common religious beliefs about death and the afterlife are a) in sharp contrast with masses of evidence and testimony consistently coming to us from different lines of investigation, and, especially, b) quite unhelpful for a person who is facing death or grieving the loss of a loved one.

I feel passionately about this problem, since a few years ago I had the painful experience of accompanying my dearest friend in a three year dramatic battle with cancer. What was painful was certainly not being at my friend's side during those difficult times. Rather, I consider that a very enriching experience. I simply cannot stand the idea that he died an anguished man. A committed Catholic, he was convinced that he was to face judgment for sins he believed he had committed.

At that time, I already knew that we have no evidence whatsoever for this kind of judgment. All the testimony we have, from a bewildering range of sources, consistently speaks of a life review instead, in which we are not "judged" by others, but rather we are helped to make sense of the life we lived, understanding ourselves what was good and what was not so good. Especially, we have not the tiniest evidence in support of support of things like Hell or eternal damnation. We appear to learn, sometimes painfully, and then to progress.

Similar in many ways is the case of a neighbour – a lovely lady in her early fifties, who looks more like a woman in her seventies. For years, she's been grieving the premature death of her husband, and this has taken a big toll on her mind and body. When I said that I knew things that perhaps could help relieve some of her grief, she listened to me politely for a while, but then she said that she could not entertain the idea of survival, and, especially, of after-death communication, because of her religious thinking.

In all honesty, this makes me angry. If religions, as Karl Marx famously said, are people's opium, then they should make people feel good, or at least not so bad. They should certainly not add to the load of suffering connected with death and dying.

Furthermore, there is the problem of confusion, contradictions, lack of clarity. I was raised a bland Catholic by a moderately religious family. That's the reason why I focus on Christianity/Catholicism here – I do not single that particular religion out or make any value judgment. The fact is, I am pretty convinced that if you were to ask ten Catholic or Christian people for a description of what happens after they die, you would get ten different answers. Where do people go before resurrection? Does resurrection happen for everybody? Do bad people go to hell immediately, or after judgment day? Do you have to be first resurrected and then, if bad, go to Hell? What happens if you are bad and repent? Where is, in the sequence of events, Purgatory? Etc.

I suspect that many teachings of religion may look absurd, inconsistent, incoherent, even to the faithful. Many others are partially known or poorly understood (ask churchgoers to give you an explanation of the exact meaning of many of the things said every Sunday by the priest during Holy Mass, and you're in for a surprise). And still, people cling to these beliefs with fervour. That's what they've been taught – understandable or not, reasonable or not, comforting or not – and that's what they believe.

With the help of a great article by Miles Edward Allen, let's focus for a moment on the belief that speaking with the dead is sinful.

The main support for this belief in the Old Testament is from the book known as Leviticus. The key verse says "Do not turn to mediums or wizards, do not seek them out to be defiled by them". There is another verse in Leviticus and one in Deuteronomy that clearly judge those who make a practice of talking to dead people: "A man or a woman who is a medium or a wizard shall be put to death" and "There shall not be found among you any one who … is a medium, for they are an abomination to the Lord".

There can be no doubt that these statements are in the Bible and that they distinctly prohibit consultations with the spirit world. If you accept Leviticus and Deuteronomy as the unerring word of the Almighty, then you would be wise to avoid any contact with mediums. But, before you make such a decision, you might want to know what else you are signing up for.

Have you ever eaten a rare steak? Or a fatty hamburger? Have you ever trimmed your hair or beard? Did you ever get a tattoo; peak at your brother in the nude; fail to stand when an old man enters the room? Have you ever worn a shirt of cotton and polyester blend? Perhaps you have cursed a politician? According to the Old Testament, all these acts, and many, many others, are sins against the Lord and are condemned just as strongly as consulting a medium.

Finally, and this is even more difficult to accept, some of the teachings do not even allegedly come from God. For instance, the ultimate nature of Christ and other essential aspects of the doctrine were decided upon by vote amongst bishops, most importantly during the Council of Nicaea in 325CE.

Now this may really seem like a tirade against religion, and Christianity in particular. It is not. It is a tirade against the unnecessary suffering deriving from uncritically accepting and believing some – at times poorly understood – religious teachings. Teachings in support of which there is no evidence whatsoever. Evidence from psychical research points to an entirely different view about life and the afterlife. However, I am certainly not advocating for switching one belief for another. My strong advice is to consider the evidence, study it, reflect upon it. Use your intelligence, your reason, and draw your own conclusions from the data. Chances are, as medical research proves, you will emerge with a clearer – and extraordinarily more comforting – understanding of death and the afterlife.

Chapter three

Bases for a rational belief in life after life

As I said in the introduction, this book has two main aims. First, I would like to establish the credibility of some of the major sources of information we have on the process of death and on the nonmaterial dimension where we allegedly continue our existence after having shed the material body – what we call the spirit world, or the afterlife if you prefer. Then, once we are reasonably confident that our sources are real and trustworthy, we can launch ourselves into trying to map this complex realm of nonmaterial existence, with its multiple levels and – apparently – the possibility for reincarnation.

However, the main sources of information we'll be using for our mapping exercise (to each of which I will devote a substantive, in-depth chapter) represent only a fraction of what I call a "sea of evidence" for the "unbelievable truth" I spoke about in the introduction. The fact that, in a way we do not yet understand, human personality appears to survive the death of the physical body is in fact supported by a much larger set of empirical evidence, huge both in terms of quantity and of diversity. In this last introductory chapter, I would like to better explain what I mean by evidence, and provide at least a bird's eye view of the dozen or so fields of investigation in which evidence for life after life has been collected by some of the finest scientific minds of the planet for nearly 200 years. Essentially, here I am going to lay the foundations: I will explain to you why I think that, based on the evidence, a rational person can believe in the afterlife. In later chapters, we will "zoom in" on our privileged sources of information.

What do we mean by evidence?

So, let's begin by getting a better idea of what evidence is. According to the Oxford English Dictionary, evidence is "the available body of facts or information indicating whether a belief or proposition is true or valid." Since what we are considering here is the belief or proposition that life continues after the demise of the body, what does the "available body of facts or information" consist of that proves the proposition is true?

Broadly speaking, I classify evidence in three main categories, and these are of different sizes. In order to visualise their respective proportions, it is useful to think of a pyramid. Imagine a pyramid sliced horizontally roughly half-way up. It is obvious that the bottom part is much larger in volume than the top part. Then think of slicing again the top part of the pyramid into two sections: the top part, where the apex is, will contain less volume, and the bottom part a bit more. These proportions represent quite realistically the quantity of evidence we have in the three main categories.

So, starting at the bottom, we find the vast majority of the evidence: facts and information. These come in the form of anecdotes, that is the stories people tell about experiences they had, or things they witnessed. People, for example, say they see apparitions of the deceased – a lot of people, in fact. Many other people report having had an evidential reading with a medium, who reported information about a deceased loved one that he or she could not possibly have acquired by normal means. Unfortunately, the obtuse sceptics have always stubbornly refused to consider anecdotes as a reliable source of information. This is a serious logical and methodological mistake in science, one they should be called to account for.

As a matter of principle, as a general attitude in life, I do believe what people say. In particular, as a medical doctor, what patients tell me, their stories, are extremely important to me. Collecting them is a fundamental part of the process of making a diagnosis and choosing a therapy. Imagine if I were to discard my patients' stories as a source of reliable information. Furthermore, the entire judicial system relies on people's testimony. Based on the words of a witness in a court of law, a person can be sentenced to death or set free. If we did not trust the accounts people give, the entire edifice of the judicial system would crumble.

Now, obviously, we should not commit the opposite – and equally damaging – mistake, the one of believing *a priori* anything people say. Rarely, people may lie. Much more frequently, they may be victims of delusions, or perceptual errors. For this reason, I do not consider anecdotes as "proof" of anything. I just say that I tend to believe them, and I am open to consider them as one of the elements of evidence in a broader context. In particular, they are great "pointers" - a sort of destination board pointing researchers towards areas that may require further investigation.

Before leaving anecdotes, thinking that they are just interesting stories and carry little weight, we have to consider some practicalities. Let's remember that, particularly concerning stories having to do with the so-called "paranormal", a) people have no incentive whatsoever to lie (most people, in fact, are reticent to relate such stories for fear of ridicule), and b) there is generally no proof or evidence that they lied.

Furthermore, when people not only tell stories, but put their accounts in writing and sign them as testimony in the course of an investigation, I am even more disposed to consider them as evidence. Finally, when you've got completely unrelated people, in different parts of the world and different epochs, who tell the same kind of stories, then I get really interested. Even more so when you have a group of people who witness the same unusual event and give accounts which are perfectly in accordance with each other, and every one of them signs written statements.

In summary, under the right circumstances (when they don't fear ridicule), people of all walks of life tell all sorts of "paranormal" stories, many of which imply survival of personality after bodily death. These stories are in the thousands, hundreds of thousands, possibly millions. There are dozens of carefully collected anthologies, in which the accounts of anomalous events are dated and signed like official documents. The volume of evidence coming from anecdotes is therefore huge, and they rightly take up the most part of the pyramid I used as an example. BUT, admittedly, their "weight" in determining whether the proposition that we don't die is true is relatively smaller.

The next section of the pyramid has proportionately less evidence, but that particular evidence carries considerably more weight. We are talking of investigations, which are typically carried out in a naturalistic setting, that is where and when the phenomena take place.

Often alerted by what are technically called "spontaneous cases" – anecdotes about some happening that looks really interesting – investigators go and try to observe the phenomena. Please remember that investigators are generally professionally trained scientists, well versed in the techniques of field research and often with many years of experience.

A typical example would be an alleged manifestation of physical mediumship. Stories would begin to circulate about a certain medium who not only delivers evidential messages allegedly coming from the deceased, but seems to be able to produce a range of astonishing physical phenomena (including voices appearing out of thin air, movement of objects, extraordinary luminous phenomena and in some cases the production of the mysterious substance called ectoplasm).

If the anecdotes are numerous and credible enough, a group of scientists (typically under the aegis of one of the professional associations such as the Society for Psychical Research) may decide to go and observe the phenomena by themselves. In doing so, they apply as many controls as feasible to eliminate the possibility of fraud or deception (you would not believe the extremes they go to do so); they record their observations with various methods, including audio and video recording; they collect statements from the other witnesses; finally, in producing a report of the investigation, they carefully consider possible alternative explanations for what they have witnessed and recorded. You will understand, then, that the relative "weight" of the evidence produced by investigations is much higher. We could consider investigations as "professionally validated anecdotes".

Finally, at the top of the pyramid, we find laboratory experiments. These are relatively few, but carry the most weight. In the laboratory, researchers have complete control over *all* the parameters - they can test particular hypotheses, and eliminate all other factors. One example would be, "Can research mediums provide accurate, specific, detailed information about a deceased person when no communication whatsoever with the sitter is possible?" The answer, as we will see in a later chapter, is a definite yes. What you must understand is that, in this example, the scientists really have control on *all* the parameters of the experiment: if the experiment is well designed, we can be 100% sure that the information the medium provides could not, under any circumstance, have been acquired through "normal" means.

Furthermore, the strength of the laboratory evidence is multiplied by what we call replications. The latest round of mediumship experiments, for instance, have been replicated five times, using the same methodology, by different groups of researchers in different parts of the world, and have all produced the same results. In science, this normally amounts to *proof*. Period. When you have several independent replications of an experiment demonstrating a given effect, the effect is considered as proven.

Does any particular piece of evidence "prove" the existence of the afterlife?

No, in my personal view, that is not the case. The *unbelievable truth* that we are talking about is so essentially incredible that I personally do not consider any single element, no matter how strong, as proof. Rather, my rational belief in an afterlife is based on the *collective weight* of the evidence. When you have a very large number of pieces of evidence all consistently pointing in the same direction, then a belief based on reason is justified.

This concept has been presented through many analogies. I always liked the one of the bamboo sticks. Let's say that you have to go across a ditch, and you only have one bamboo stick that you can lay across. The stick looks sturdy, very solid, and perhaps could carry your weight. But perhaps not? Also, you would have to balance yourself very delicately not to fall off that single stick. If you had two, their carrying strength would be doubled, and you could place one foot on each stick for better balance. Still, if you wanted to make sure not to fall into the mud at the bottom of the ditch, you would want more. With ten sticks, you could walk across very comfortably. Now, if every piece of evidence produced by psychical research in the last couple of hundred years were a bamboo stick, you could go across the ditch *with an armoured tank!* Many of these sticks are sturdy and super solid, many are OK, and, inevitably, some are less reliable. But the bamboo sticks are so spectacularly many that, taken together, they could carry an enormous weight: they can safely take anybody willing to do so from incredulity and disbelief to what I keep calling a rational belief in life after life.

What is all this evidence telling us?

And here we come to the crucial point, the core subject of this entire course. What does all this evidence tell us? How do anecdotes, investigation and laboratory research in many different and diverse fields all contribute to forming a coherent picture? In order to answer this question, we should look at a very brief, essential description of these fields of research.

First of all, we have parapsychology research, which tells us without reasonable doubt that we *do* have psychic powers. In particular, thousands upon thousands of carefully designed experiments carried out by universities around the world, amounting to a total of many *millions* of individual trials, confirm that:

- We can have transfer of information between individuals when all known channels of communication are closed - this is called *telepathy*.

- We can be conscious of events happening in another place - what is called *remote viewing* - and in another time, the future in particular - this is called *precognition*.

- Our minds can have a direct influence on inanimate matter and living organisms - this is called *psychokinesis*.

Although the existence of these psychic powers is not directly related to the survival hypothesis (the *unbelievable truth*), we have to give it serious consideration, because it shows that the equation mind equals physical brain is false. If psychic powers are real, then the mind is necessarily *more* than the physical brain. And this is very important, because when we understand that mind is related to, but independent of the physical brain, then we can be more open to consider the survival hypothesis.

Then we push the envelope further, and we do so by looking at evidence that points to mind functioning outside the physical body - these are called *out of body experiences, or OBEs*. Here too, we have considerable anecdotal evidence. Dozens of books have been written by people who claim that they can leave their body at will, and there even is a respected institution (the Monroe Institute in the US) which has, for decades, been running courses to teach people to move their consciousness out of their bodies. And we have some laboratory experimental evidence as well, perhaps not much in terms of volume, but certainly striking in terms of results. OBEs are important for the survival hypothesis because they not only show that mind and consciousness are independent of the physical brain, but also that they don't even need a physical body to exist and function!

Thirdly, and most importantly, we must look at mind functioning when the physical brain is actually dead. This is a fundamental piece in the entire puzzle, and will be the subject of a whole in-depth chapter in this book. In short, the quantity, quality and strength of the evidence from what we call *Near-Death Experiences* or NDEs is simply colossal. In thousands upon thousands of well researched and documented eases, people who are clinically dead - people with *no functioning brain whatsoever*, for 10, 15 or 20 minutes - are later resuscitated by medical intervention and report a very complex and very similar conscious experience. Suffice to say that every one – I mean every single one – of the medical researchers who have dedicated their life to the study of this incredible phenomenon is convinced that it is highly suggestive of life after life.

Fourthly, we have the so-called *Deathbed Visions*. In another in-depth chapter of this book we will learn that, of the 10% of people who are conscious at the moment of their death, as many as *two thirds* have visions of what appears to be the afterlife, and of deceased relatives, who are constantly said to have come to "take them over".

Fifthly, we have very solid evidence from *reincarnation* studies. Much of it comes from the study and painstaking investigation of thousands of cases of children, all over the world, who remember a previous life in stunning, inexplicable details. This area of research was pioneered for over 30 years by prof. Ian Stevenson of the Division of Perceptual Studies at the University of Virginia, and is currently pursued by several other researchers. The idea of reincarnation, however, is also supported by regression hypnosis, originally developed by Dr Brian Weiss and now used by dozens of therapists, both for research and as a form of psychotherapy.

Lastly, we have an ocean within the larger ocean of evidence. This is *after death communication*, the fact that the world of the living appears to interact with the world of the so called dead. The evidence in this area is so much, and so diverse, that it is convenient to break it down in sub-categories, which are proper areas of investigation in their own right:

- *Apparitions* – these are basically ghost stories, when people – individuals, but also groups – see the apparition of a dead person. This includes alleged hauntings and the very intriguing phenomenon of poltergeists.

- *Mediumship* – mental and physical mediumship, and automatic writing – for which we have an incredible amount of anecdotes, thorough investigations and good, solid laboratory experiments. Discarnate personalities (spirits, in common parlance) communicating with us through mediums are the third main source of information we will use to attempt a "mapping" of the afterlife. Mediumship will therefore be dealt with in depth in a later chapter.

- *Instrumental Trans-Communication* or ITC, which consists of what appears as communication – at times even two-way communication – with discarnate personalities through technological means such as tape recorders, radios, television and others. Here too, the amount of evidence and the diversity of the techniques which have been successfully employed for the last 70 years should grant ITC its own division in sub-categories.

- *Induced After-Death Communication* or IADC, which consists of a range of psychological techniques successfully employed to facilitate the direct communication between grieving people and their deceased loved ones. These techniques, initially pioneered by clinical psychologist Alan Botkin and celebrity researcher and author Dr Raymond Moody, have been thoroughly studied in the laboratory and have rates of success varying between 20 and over 60 percent according to different studies. IADC is now increasingly used as a therapeutic intervention to support grief recovery.

Consistency is the key

When looking at these diverse areas of evidence, is important to realise that they *all* point in the same direction. It is the *consistency* of anecdotes, investigation and laboratory research produced about different phenomena, in different parts of the world, for the best part of the last 200 years and under the most diverse conditions imaginable, that provides what I consider proof.

Interestingly, an Australian lawyer, Victor Zammit, engaged in a remarkable study some years ago. He looked at the evidence we very briefly outlined above and considered, in legal procedural terms, if a) it would be admissible in a court of law, and b) if it could influence the verdict of a jury. His conclusion was that *even a small fraction of the available evidence would be of sufficient strength for a jury to issue a unanimous verdict*. If the jurors were asked "Can mind, consciousness and personality exist independently of the physical body?", the verdict would be a unanimous "Yes". And if the same jurors were asked "Can we hold a rational belief that death as we commonly understand it does not exist, and that after the demise of the physical body we go on living in a nonmaterial, spiritual dimension?", the answer would equally be a resounding "Yes".

This does not need to be a contemporary jury, however. This verdict has already been issued over a century ago, by some of the finest intellects at the time. Already then, after having studied only a fraction of the evidence we have today, the founding fathers of the Society for Psychical Research in the UK had drawn their conclusions. It is in 1904 that Cambridge University professor Frederic Myers, whom many of us consider almost as an intellectual father figure, captured all this in the classic of the classics – *Human Personality and its Survival of Bodily Death*.

Chapter four

What are Near-Death Experiences and why is it reasonable to trust them?

In today's world, the only way not to be aware of the phenomenon called Near-Death Experiences (from now on, for brevity, "NDEs") is probably to have grown up – and still live – in the Amazon forest or in the desert of Namibia. Since the publication of Dr Raymond Moody's *Life After Life* in 1977, the whole world has been taken by storm by these accounts of most extraordinary, joyous, uplifting and life-transforming experiences. NDE experiencers (from now on, "NDEers") have written innumerable books, and have appeared on countless radio, TV and press interviews. The subject has been debated to exhaustion, between sceptics, who will systematically ignore the evidence and regurgitate "explanations" that have been disproven time and again, and the real medical researchers, scientists who have dedicated their lives to the study of this phenomenon and are invariably – *all of them* – convinced that it is highly suggestive of life after life. NDEs are so popular that even a few Hollywood films have been made with them as a core subject.

A question remains, however, especially for somebody who is at the same time in fear of death and in fear of being "taken for a ride" by believing something that may appear too good to be true. The vast majority of NDE accounts describe the experience as the best one can possibly have. Study after study show that NDEers are literally transformed by the experience, with a number of permanent, beneficial changes in their psychology, beliefs and behaviour. First and foremost among those changes is that any fear of death is completely erased. These people have directly experienced the afterlife and only wait to go back into the light. Can this possibly be true? Are these people describing a real experience, or a dream based on their desires? How "dead" were they when they had this experience? Essentially, and crucially, can we trust their testimony?

This is going to be a long chapter. In order to answer the last essential and crucial question, I will have to tell you about the science of NDEs – what empirical evidence tells us, and why it is reasonable to trust the testimony of NDErs concerning life after life. I will try to do that in the simplest possible terms, and yet there is quite a mass of information that you will have to go through. I encourage you to follow me with attention, for another piece of research shows something truly remarkable.

In the mid-1980s, Dr Kenneth Ring, Professor Emeritus of psychology at the University of Connecticut, published research showing that many of the beneficial changes I briefly mentioned above – notably including the disappearance of the fear of death – show up in people who have *not* had an NDE, but simply read about them. The more people read, research and study this fascinating subject, the greater the extent of the changes. Therefore, I promise you that if you will dedicate the necessary attention to what I am going to say over the next pages, you will experience a noticeable lift in your mood, and a decrease in your fear. Knowledge is indeed power!

A peek into the world to come

Before getting into the substance, let's look at what can be considered a fairly typical NDE account, just to remind us of what a prodigious experience this really is. Interestingly, we are looking at something that happened well before NDEs became popular, which dispels the persistent myth that NDErs imagine their experience based on accounts they've heard in the media or read about. In fact, NDEs have been reported in essentially the same terms by all races, cultures and spiritual traditions throughout history, with the earliest accounts dating back some 3,000 years!

From the *St Louis Medical and Surgical Journal* we learn that, in 1889, physician A.S. Wiltse contracted typhoid fever and, after a short period in which his conditions deteriorated quickly, was considered dead by those who were caring for him. These included a physician, who failed to trigger any reaction from Wiltse by jabbing a needle in various parts of his body. For four hours, Wiltse appeared dead, without a pulse or detectable heartbeat. Later, Fredric Myers and Edmund Gurney, among the founders of the British Society for Psychical Research, obtained sworn statements from the witnesses, all agreeing on the fact that Wiltse appeared to have died. In reality, while lying lifeless on the bed, Wiltse recalls being about to emerge from the body and appearing to himself like a jellyfish in colour and form. He had the sensation of floating up and down and laterally like a soap bubble attached to the end of a pipe, until

> "I broke free from the body ... and fell lightly on the floor, where I slowly rose and expanded into the full stature of a man. I seemed to be translucent, of a bluish cast, and perfectly naked. As I turned, my elbow came into contact with the arm of one of two gentlemen who were standing in the door. To my surprise, his arm passed through mine without apparent resistance, the severed parts closing again without pain, as air reunites. I looked quickly up at his face, to see if whether he had noticed the contact, but he gave no sign ... I directed my gaze in the direction of his, and saw my own dead body. It was laying just as I had taken so much pain to place it, partially on the right side, the feet close together, and the

hands clasped across the breast ... I was surprised at the paleness of the face ... and saw a number of people sitting or standing about the body ... and ... attempted to gain the attention of the people with them as well as reassuring them of my own immortality ... I passed among them, but found they gave me no heed ... I concluded that they "are watching what they think is I, but they are mistaken." That is not I. This is I and I am as much alive as ever. How well I feel, though. Only a few minutes ago I was horribly sick and distressed. Then came the change called death which I have so much dreaded. This has passed now, and here I am, still a man, still alive and thinking, yes thinking as clearly as ever, and how well I feel: I shall never be sick again. I have no more to die."

The physician then describes a sensation of upwardly movement, independent of his will, eventually finding himself in another world, in which he encounters some sort of barrier. He communicates with an unknown presence, telling him that if he crosses that barrier he will not be able to go back. The question is then asked whether Wiltse believes his task on Earth is finished. After deciding that it is not, "Without previous thought and without apparent effort on my part, my eyes opened. I looked at my hands and then at the little white cot upon which I was lying and realising that I was in the body, and in astonishment and disappointment, I exclaimed 'What in the world has happened to me? Must I die again?'"

If you don't know much about NDEs, this account looks wondrous. A person in a state of apparent death, or at least deeply unconscious, to the point of not responding to repeated painful stimulation, has a fully conscious experience, which is remembered in fine details. In this experience, Dr Wiltse finds himself out of his body, and yet still has the feeling of having a body, even if immaterial. He explicitly says that nothing changed in his feeling of being alive, his thinking, his emotions. If we are to believe this short account, death is nothing but a transition. Life continues almost exactly as before, only in a nonmaterial dimension – one which, at least in the beginning, is very close to the material reality which has been left behind.

On the other hand, if you do know about NDEs, Dr Wiltse's account is perhaps not fully satisfactory. Where are all the "spiritual", fully otherworldly components that so frequently appear in the accounts of the NDErs? Yes, because for many, temporarily stepping into what appears to be the afterlife is a mesmerising experience of light, warmth, unconditional love, acceptance, higher learning, wisdom and bliss. It is time, then, to bring all readers "up to speed", so to say, so that we all know rather precisely what we mean when we talk of NDEs. Once that is done, we will look at the evidence showing that such experiences indicate that our mind can exist and function independently from the physical body, and that NDEs are likely to be what they appear – a foray into the afterlife.

Who's having NDEs?

The first question we may ask is, how common are NDEs? Measurements and estimates vary widely. Without annoying you with references to the plethora of studies carried out in different countries, let me tell you that when individuals in the general population are asked, between 4% and 15% report having had an NDE. Although these numbers may seem low, remember that they refer to *everybody* in the population. These data indicate that an astonishingly high proportion of the population experiences a near death experience and that this phenomenon is most probably quite common, certainly far more common than most had originally thought. Then, when studies consider individuals who have actually come close to death (such as after a cardiac arrest, for example), the percentages go up significantly. In the US, Kenneth Ring found that some 30% of those individuals report an NDE and his estimate closely matches the 27% found by American Cardiologist Michael Sabom. An English study found 10%, and a

Dutch study looking specifically at cardiac arrest patients found that 12% had a deep NDE.

You may wonder why such percentages vary, and more in general, if this is a real phenomenon, why doesn't *everybody* who comes close to death have an NDE. These are logical and pertinent questions and remain largely unanswered. We must be honest and admit that, if on the one hand we have many reasons to believe the phenomenon reflects a real experience, on the other there are many things we don't know or understand yet. However, there are a couple of interesting considerations to make. First, we know for a fact that we all dream at night, in fact several times every night. And yet, it is everybody's experience that we only remember a fraction of our dreams, and at times none at all. It is therefore reasonable to think that everybody who comes that close to death has an NDE, but a relatively small and variable percentage actually remembers it. Secondly, and more importantly, studies indicate that the likelihood of having an NDE is much higher in patients who were actually close to irreversible death – the most serious and severe the clinical situation, the more likely the patient is to have an NDE. This, interestingly, has been shown to be the case particularly in children. It would therefore appear that we are allowed to take a peek into the world of spirit when we are close to crossing the threshold of no return.

A complex, highly structured experience

Now, let's look at what the experience actually consists of. Like two persons will never be completely identical, no two NDEs are absolutely equal. There are, however, a number of common, recurrent themes. We'll look later at how often the following themes, or components, are reported by NDErs. For the moment let's say that if at least six of them are reported, the NDE is classified as "core" or "deep". In the following list, each theme is followed by a representative example, each one picked from a different account amid the gigantic literature available on the subject.

1. A sensation of floating out of one's body - often followed by an out-of-body experience where all that goes on around the "vacated" body is both seen and heard accurately.

   "All of a sudden, I noticed a floating sensation, as if I were rising. I was shocked to find that I was floating upwards into the open air above the river. I remember vividly the scene of the water level passing before my eyes. Suddenly I could hear and see like never before. The sound of the waterfall was so crisp and clear that it cannot be explained by words. Earlier that year, my right ear had been injured. But now I could hear perfectly clearly, better than I ever had before. My sight was even more beautiful. Sights that were close in distance were as clear as those far away, and this was at the same moment, which astounded me. There was no blurriness in my vision whatsoever. I felt as if I had been limited by my physical senses all these years, and that I had been looking at a distorted picture of reality.

   As I floated there about six feet above the water, I gazed downwards towards the falls. I knew that my physical body was eight feet below the surface of the water, but it did not seem to bother me... Now, separated from my physical body, I found that I could survive without all the pain and suffering of physical existence. I had never thought of it as pain and suffering when I was in my physical body, but now, after experiencing such total bliss and harmony, it seemed like everything prior to this was like being in some sort of cage."

2. A sense of otherworldly peace.

> "I travelled to another realm of total and absolute peace . There was no pain, but instead a sense of well-being, in a dark, soft space. I was enveloped by total bliss in an atmosphere of unconditional love and acceptance. The darkness was beautiful and stretching on and on. The freedom of total peace was intensified beyond any ecstatic feeling ever felt here on earth. In the distance, I saw a horizon of whitish, yellowish light. I find it very difficult to describe where I was, because the words we know here in this plane aren't adequate enough."

3. Passing through a dark tunnel, or black hole, or encountering some kind of darkness. This is often accompanied by a feeling or sensation of movement or acceleration. "Wind" may be heard or felt.

> "I remember going through a tunnel, a very, very dark tunnel ... A very vast one. It started at a narrow point and became wider and wider. But I remember it being very very black. I wasn't afraid because I knew there was something at the other end waiting for me that was good ... I found it very pleasant. I wasn't afraid or anything. There was no fear attached to it. I felt very light. I felt I was floating."

4. Ascending toward a light at the end of the darkness - a light of incredible brilliance, with the possibility of seeing people, animals, plants, lush outdoors, and even cities within the light.

> "Gradually the earth scene faded away, and through it loomed a bright, new, beautiful world - beautiful beyond imagination! For half a minute I

could see both worlds at once. Finally, when the earth was all gone, I stood in a glory that could only be heaven.

In the background were two beautiful, round-topped mountains, similar to Fujiyama in Japan. The tops were snowcapped, and the slopes were adorned with foliage of indescribable beauty. The mountains appeared to be about fifteen miles away, yet I could see individual flowers growing on their slopes. I estimated my vision to be about one hundred times better than on earth.

To the left was a shimmering lake containing a different kind of water - clear, golden, radiant, and alluring. It seemed to be alive. The whole landscape was carpeted with grass so vivid, clear, and green, that it defies description. To the right was a grove of large, luxuriant trees, composed of the same clear material that seemed to make up everything."

5. Greeted by friendly voices, people or beings who may be strangers, deceased loved ones, or religious figures. Conversation can ensue, information or a message may be given.

"I awakened from the surgery and was blinded by a river of white light. I thought it was an aftereffect of the general anesthesia. I thought it was odd that it pushed beyond my optic nerve and went through my entire body. I immediately rose to my feet and looked at the nurse who had helped me up.

She wasn't a nurse. She was clothed in light, extraordinarily beautiful and loving. She was the most beautiful woman I had ever seen, and I almost cry when I think about it. She wore a loose-fitting white gown, and it gave off light of its own ... The light around her was flooding into me, and seemed to pour into everything ... The light that shone from the centre of her was gloriously beautiful, This light, combined with her colouring, had an astonishing impact on me. The facial features were overpowered by this inner radiance. I could literally feel her love and care ... I had the impression that she knew me very well, and that I was very familiar to her, but she didn't say.

I looked back and down at my body, still lying on the recovery couch under a blanket. Here I was, standing beside a being of light, and looking at my body. Something seemed wrong.

She led me off to the side, and I again looked back at my body, lying in the couch. She had a veil of energy to her back. It separated her world from mine ... I understood immediately that I wasn't allowed to go through there. She said 'It's a one-way path. If you go through there, you can't come back here. Your life will be over, and you won't have done the things you need to do.' Brilliant shards of light in all colours danced around the opening. They appeared and disappeared, as if the light energy was being fragmented and shattered at the point of contact between two worlds at different energy levels."

6. Seeing a panoramic review of the life just lived, from birth to death or in reverse order, sometimes becoming a reliving of the life rather than a dispassionate viewing. The person's life can be reviewed in its entirety or in segments. This is usually accompanied by a feeling or need to assess loss or gains during the life to determine what was learned or not learned. Other

beings can take part in this judgment, e.g. through offering advice.

> "Mine was not a review but a reliving. For me, it was a total reliving of every thought I had ever thought, every word I had ever spoken, and every deed I had ever done; plus the effect of each thought, word and deed on everyone and anyone who had ever come within my environment or sphere of influence, whether I knew them or not."

7. Entering into the Light.

> "I felt as I was moving at the speed of light through the blackness, and far away in the distance I could see a small pinpoint of light that seemed to be growing larger. I somehow knew that this was my destination. I sped along until it became a huge mass of beautiful and brilliant white light. I stopped short right before reaching it, for I felt I was getting too far away from earth to find my way back, and I guess I had the feeling of what one could equate with homesickness.
>
> As I sat there motionless, it seemed as if the light began to float towards me as if to take up the slack. It was not long before it engulfed me, and I felt as if I became one with the light. It seemed to have knowledge of everything there is to know, and it accepted me as part of it. I felt all-knowing for a few minutes. Suddenly, everything seemed to make perfect sense. The whole world seemed in total harmony. I remember thinking 'Ahhh, so that's it. Everything is so crystal clear and simple in so many ways.' I had never been able to see it from this point of view.
>
> Looking back at this point, I cannot explain the questions that were answered, or the answers

themselves. All I know was that they were on a much higher level of thought that cannot be approached when limited by the physical nature of the mind ... Within the light, I could still feel the boundaries of my form, but at the same time I felt as one with it. I felt myself expand through the light over an area that seemed like miles, and the contract to my former size. I felt better than I had ever felt in my life. It was as if I were bathing in total love and understanding, and basking in its radiance ... It gives me a sense of travelling a long distance and finally making it home. I sensed that I had been here before, perhaps before being born in the physical world."

8. A reluctance to return to the earth plane, but invariably realizing either their job on earth is not finished or a mission must yet be accomplished before they can return to stay.

"Then I was aware of an Immense Presence coming toward me, bathed in white, shimmering light that glowed and at times sparkled like diamonds. Everything else seen, the colours, beings, faded into the distance as the Light Being permeated everything. I was being addressed by an overwhelming presence. Even though I felt unworthy, I was being lifted into that which I could embrace. The Joy and Ecstasy were intoxicating. It was 'explained' that I could remain there if I wanted; it was a choice I could make.

There was much teaching going on, and I was just 'there' silently, quietly. I felt myself expanding and becoming part of All That Was in Total Freedom Unconditionally. I became aware again that I needed to make a choice. Part of me wanted to remain forever, but I finally realized I didn't want to leave a new baby motherless. I left with sadness and reluctance."

9. Warped sense of time and space. Discovering time and space do not exist, losing the need to recognize measurements of life either as valid or necessary.

> "From the onset of this rather superconscious state of the darkness of the tunnel, there was something that was totally missing, and that was what we call time. There's no such thing as time in heaven! As I thought of and formulated a desire or a question, it would already have been recognized, acknowledged, and therefore answered. And the dialogue that took place, took place in no time. It didn't require a fifteen-minute duration in time; it simply happened."

10. Disappointment at being revived. Often feeling a need to shrink or somehow squeeze to fit back in to the physical body. There can be unpleasantness, even anger or tears at the realisation they are now back in their bodies and no longer on "The Other Side."

> "Then, instantly, I felt myself slam into my body ... At that point, I felt the most incredible, searing pain imaginable in my abdomen, all the way through my backbone ... I couldn't believe I was returned to such hellish environment, but then the beauty of the experience flooded back to me, giving me the most serene peace and calm I could hope for under the circumstances."

As I was saying earlier, no two NDEs are equal. This is not difficult to understand: imagine that ten different people visit the town of Paris, and upon return tell their experience. Would you expect them to tell exactly the same story, to highlight the same details, to use the same words? Of course not. In their accounts there would likely be many common themes – after all, they all have been to the same city – but there would be considerable variations in their stories. This is exactly what appears to be happening with NDEs. Numerous studies have looked at the relative frequency with which the main themes we just described are reported by NDErs. If we combine the results of all these studies, we come up with a table like this one:

Peace or joy	71%
Out-of-body experience	57%
Encountering a light	44%
Meeting others or a being	38%
Entering the light	33%
Entering a tunnel/dark void	30%
Life review	13%

Profound psychological and behavioural changes

Anyhow, regardless of its specific form and content, for most experiencers an NDE is an extraordinary, sublime experience. So extraordinary, in fact, that it produces in those who have had it deep and permanent changes in personality, thoughts, values and behaviours. Study after study have shown that NDErs have:

- Increased appreciation for life.
- Increased self-acceptance.
- Increased compassionate concern for others (in fact, not only for humans but for all other forms of life).
- Decreased interest for material goods.
- Decreased competitiveness.

- Increased spirituality (very interestingly, NDErs who were religious before showed a decrease in their interest for the formal aspects of religion and increased interest for a more universal and comprehensive spirituality).
- Increased interest in knowledge for its own sake.
- Sense of purpose in life.
- Virtual disappearance of the fear of death.
- Belief in life after death.
- Belief in God or in a superior being, sometimes referred to as "the Light".

Is all this for real?

At this point, we are left with an inevitable question – the nagging doubt I talked about at the beginning of the chapter. Is the NDE a "real" experience? Are NDErs really allowed a "peek" into what appears to be the afterlife, a nonmaterial, spiritual world where nonetheless we retain our thoughts, memory, perceptions and personality? For the remainder of the chapter, I will explain to you the main reasons why, as I said, virtually all the medical doctors, psychologists and other scientists who have seriously investigated the evidence are convinced that NDEs are "highly suggestive of life after life", that is the continuation of consciousness after the death of the physical body. Again, this is going to be a bit long, but I encourage you to follow with attention, for at the end it will be your reason, and not just hope or blind faith, that will give you enormous comfort.

First, then, let's spell out the core mystery, the main and astonishing issue for the NDE. In the words of Pim Van Lommel, the Dutch cardiologist author of a landmark study published in the *The Lancet*, possibly the most respected medical journal in the world, "At that moment these people are not only conscious; their consciousness is even more expansive than ever. They can think extremely clearly, have memories going back to their earliest childhood and experience an intense connection with everything and everyone around them. And yet the brain shows no activity at all!"

Dr Van Lommel, like all of us, is astounded because according to the prevailing theories in neuroscience, *any* conscious experience – and especially a highly complex experience such an NDE, involving the formation of detailed, long-lasting memories and resulting in significant psychological and behavioural changes – requires the *full functionality* and *coordination* of several units of the brain, most of which are located in the cerebral cortex. The problem is that, at the moment people have an NDE, they have *no functioning brain.*

To fully understand this, we have to look at are the best studied cases of NDE – those following cardiac arrest. Research says that NDEs can happen in a wide variety of circumstances and medical conditions. What is particularly useful in the case of cardiac arrest is that we know exactly what goes on in the brain and therefore we can assuredly say that NDErs have no functioning brain at the moment they have the experience.

When the heart stops beating and the flow of blood and oxygen to the brain drops to zero, it only takes one to two seconds for the patient to lose consciousness. It is like fainting – in a matter of just an instant one moves from full waking consciousness to what essentially is a coma. After another five to ten seconds, even the centre, deep into the brainstem, which regulates breathing, stops working. Already at that stage, with absence of heartbeat and of breathing, the person is considered clinically dead.

Soon thereafter, the whole electrical activity of the brain flatlines – it goes to zero. John Greenfield, Professor of Neurology at the University of Toledo, says, "When the brain is not getting much blood, it pretty much shuts down …. So a flat EEG typically correlates with a very inactive brain." And then he beautifully expresses the key mystery of NDEs: "In that time when it's not getting very much blood, there's really very little activity going on in the brain and it would be very unlikely that somebody could have a complex sort of dream-like state as described for most near-death experiences."

At this stage, from about 30 seconds after the heart stopped beating, even the most fundamental nervous reflexes shut down. The gagging reflex, for instance (the fact that if you touch the back of the throat you involuntarily, automatically gag), disappears. This reflex is mediated by very simple nervous structures nested deep inside the brain. The fact that it disappears indicates with certainty that not only the cerebral cortex (which is commonly believed, as we said, to be necessary for the production of consciousness) but also the deepest, oldest, most fundamental parts of the brain are off-line. People in this stage have essentially *no brain*. And yet, they report the most extraordinary experiences, which they often describe as "more real than reality", and build memories which are recalled in fine detail 20 or 25 years after the experience.

Veridical perceptions with no functioning brain

So, we have understood that people with no brain have complex experiences. This in itself is quite extraordinary, but another question arises. How do we know that these are "real" experiences and not just dreams? In order to answer that, you have to look at what NDErs report about the initial phases of the experience. When they find themselves out of their body, they often remain for a certain time in physical proximity of their "dead" body, and register many details about the environment, the people, the resuscitation procedures. As demonstrated by numerous, clever scientific studies, what NDErs report about this phase is *not* a dream or a fantasy. They report a number of exact details which, when checked against medical records, are found to be entirely correct. It indeed looks like NDErs can *see* and *hear* from a point of view outside their physical body, which, at that point, is not functioning in any way.

To give you an idea of how striking such accounts can be, let me briefly tell you the story reported in a scientific publication by Kimberly Clark, a critical care worker at Harborview Hospital in

Seattle. The case involves a woman named Maria, a migrant worker who suffered a heart attack whilst visiting relatives in Seattle and went through a cardiac arrest whilst in the coronary care unit. After having been resuscitated, Maria reported to Clark having had an NDE.

Clark, who had heard of NDEs but was sceptical of them, listened with what she described as "feigned but seemingly emphatic respect" to the patient's account of the experience. Clark reports that, inwardly, she was finding plausible explanations to dismiss the various elements of a fairly typical NDE account, until Maria mentioned something bizarre. At a certain point, Maria told Clark that she had not merely remained looking down from the ceiling, but found herself outside the hospital. Specifically, she said, having been distracted by an object on the ledge of the third floor of the north wing of the building, she "thought herself up there". And when she "arrived" she found herself, as Clark put it, "eyeball to shoelace" with – of all things – a tennis shoe on the ledge of the third floor on the north wing of the building! Maria then proceeded to describe the shoe in minute detail, mentioning, among other things, that the little toe had a worn place in the shoe, and that one of its laces was tucked underneath the heel. Maria herself got emotional, and insisted that Clark should try to locate the shoe as she desperately needed to know whether she had "really" seen it.

The north face of Harborview Hospital is slender, with only five windows showing from the third floor. When Clark arrived there, she didn't find any shoe – until she came to the middlemost window on the floor, and there, on the ledge, precisely as Maria had described it, was the tennis shoe.

The question here is: What is the probability that a migrant worker visiting a large city for the first time, who suffers a heart attack and is rushed to a hospital at night would, while having a cardiac arrest, simply "hallucinate" seeing a tennis shoe – with very specific and unusual features – on the ledge of a floor higher than her physical location at the hospital? Clark herself wrote: "The only way she could have had such a perspective was if she had been floating right outside and at very close range to the tennis shoe. I retrieved the shoe and brought it to Maria; it was very concrete evidence for me."

However, although incredibly striking, this remains a single anecdote. In order to realise that NDErs truly have veridical perceptions when out of their body we have to consider more detailed, systematic and extensive research. There have been quite a number of studies in this particular field, but they all essentially repeated the methodology and confirmed the finding of the original investigations by cardiologist Michael Sabom in the US.

The first part of the research consisted of collecting data: Sabom used detailed protocols to interview patients who reported visual experiences while undergoing cardiac surgery or in connection with cardiac arrests. He then went on to consult with members of the medical teams and other witnesses, and also examined the clinical records of these patients, in order to determine to what extent these perceptions could be verified. In most instances, Sabom was able to provide compelling evidence that these patients were reporting precise details concerning their operation, the equipment used, or characteristics of the medical personnel involved, which they could not have known about by normal means.

The second part of Dr Sabom's investigation consisted of a control procedure, devised to further test the reality of what the patients reported. He identified 25 chronic coronary care patients who had never been resuscitated, and asked them to imagine what the procedure would be like as if they were a spectator of their own resuscitation, much like the NDEers experience. The results from this control group were intriguing, to say the least. 22 of his 25 control respondents gave descriptions of their hypothetical resuscitation that were riddled with errors; their accounts were often vague, diffuse, and general, mostly based on what they remembered from TV drama. According to Sabom, the reports from patients who had actually been resuscitated and had an NDE were never marred by such errors and were considerably more detailed as well.

The blind experience vision during NDEs

Finally, the "reality" of the NDE is supported by another and even more extraordinary line of research – the study of the congenitally blind. To be clear, the International Council of Opthalmology defines congenital blindness as a complete lack of form and visual perception since birth, and is commonly referred to as no light perception, or NLP. Psychiatrist Stanislov Grof purports that sight in congenitally NDErs is medically inexplicable: "There are ... reported cases where individuals who were blind because of a medically confirmed organic damage to their optical system could at the time of clinical death see the environment ... Occurrences of this kind ... can be subjected to objective verification. They thus represent the most convincing proof that what happens in near-death experiences is more than the hallucinatory phantasmagoria of physiologically impaired brains".

In accord with Grof, psychologists Kenneth Ring and Sharon Cooper decided to conduct the most in-depth study ever undertaken of NDEs of the blind. The objective of their study was to ascertain if the blind experience the same veridical occurrences as the sighted. The blind indeed appear to see for the first time in their lives during a NDE. However, they do not retain sight when they return to their bodies. Interestingly, the research ascertained that the narratives of the blind were indistinguishable from those of the sighted. According to the two authors: "The analyses of persons blind from birth ... provide the strongest and conventionally most inexplicable data pertaining to the proposition that the blind may actually see during their NDEs."

Ring and Cooper consider "Vicki" to be one of the most compelling and verifiable cases of the congenitally blind ever recorded. Vicki was born blind due to severe and irreversible optic nerve damage. Asked in an interview if she has ever been able to see, she replied, "Nothing, never. No light, no shadows, no nothing, ever ... I've never been able to understand even the concept of light." Thus, the visual components of her NDE are astonishing. After a near-fatal car accident and suffering from brain damage, Vicki was rushed to the hospital in a coma. She recalls her experience by stating:

"And it was frightening because I'm not accustomed to see things visually, because I never had before! And initially it was pretty scary! And then I finally recognized my wedding ring and my hair. And then I thought: is that my body down there? Am I dead or what? They kept saying, 'We can't bring her back, we can't bring her back!' And they were trying to frantically work on this thing that I discovered was my body and I felt very detached from it and sort of 'so what?' And I was thinking, what are these people getting so upset about?"

Upon resuscitation Vicki described seeing her crumpled Volkswagen van. Additionally, she "saw" herself floating above the stretcher and travelling to the hospital's roof, where she experienced a 360-degree panoramic view of the hospital grounds. Vicki's surgical team later verified her accurate description of the wedding ring and precise account of both the hospital grounds and damage to her Volkswagen van.

"Normal" explanations do not stand up to scrutiny

So, you may wonder, what else would we need, after looking at this massive amount of empirical evidence, to believe, rationally believe, that NDEs are indeed a true experience? What else would we need in order to accept the testimony of NDErs as a trustworthy indication of what happens when our bodies cease to function? Well, in fact, for most people, what we described should be ample enough. However, there are hardcore sceptics who are constitutionally incapable of accepting the reality of the phenomenon, primarily because it implies that mind and consciousness can exist without a functioning brain. These sceptics, some of whom have made a career out of negating the reality of NDEs and the evidence from parapsychology in general, have for decades tried to "explain away" the NDE with a handful of theories which have been thoroughly discredited, and yet periodically resurface on the popular press under titles like "Mystery of NDEs solved." I will now briefly tell you about the most popular of such theories, so, if you come across them in the press or in talking with friends, you will be able to explain why they don't work.

First and foremost, critics say that NDEs are inventions. People just fantasise. And they imagine such things because nowadays almost everybody has heard of such experiences. You will remember me saying that there are tons of books on the subject out there, and even a couple of Hollywood movies. So, please, read the following description:

> "I was still in the room, but instead of being sick in my bed I left my body and floated up to the ceiling. I saw my body like a dead pig dressed in my clothes. My children wept over me, and this caused me intense pain. I tried to talk to my family, but no one could hear me."

I think that this has quite a number of the core elements of the near-death experience. Well, this was written *almost 500 years ago,* by an aristocrat in rural Tibet. That is more than a few years before Dr Moody's bestseller *Life After Life,* and long before Hollywood movies.

The first conclusion that we can draw, then, is that NDE reports are not limited to the modern world. In fact, descriptions of this experience – often using exactly the same words as we hear today – can be found in the literature of ancient Greece and Mesopotamia, some 30 centuries ago.

Secondly, critics say that NDEs are projections of what people expect to see in a hypothetical afterlife, or what they want to see. In reality, tons of research demonstrate that there is *no correlation* between the religious beliefs of the person and the likelihood, depth and content of the near death experience he or she may have. In fact, the likelihood, depth and content of the NDE are not correlated with age, race, sexual orientation or economic status. According to the evidence, the NDE truly appears as a universal human experience.

The next line of defence by the materialists and the sceptics is that NDEs are just hallucinations produced by a dying brain. Here again, the theory does not match the *facts*. Hallucinations are usually illogical, fleeting, bizarre, and/or distorted, whereas the vast majority of NDEs are logical, orderly, clear, and comprehensible. People tend to forget their hallucinations, whereas most NDEs remain vivid for decades. NDEs often lead to profound and permanent transformations in personality, attitudes, beliefs and values, something that is never seen following hallucinations. People looking back on hallucinations typically recognize them as unreal, as fantasies, whereas, people often describe their NDEs as "more real than real." Finally, people who have experienced both hallucinations and an NDE describe them as being quite different.

The next most popular sceptic explanation is that the phenomenon is cause by falling levels of oxygen in the brain - what is technically known as hypoxia. Well, first of all, the symptoms of hypoxia have *nothing to do* with the content of a near death experience. Secondly, physicians have compared oxygen levels of cardiac arrest survivors who did and did not have NDEs and their findings discredit the anoxia hypothesis. In fact, in one study, the NDErs had higher oxygen levels than non-NDErs.

Another explanation looks at the blood levels of another gas, carbon dioxide. As breathing stops and oxygen levels go down, carbon dioxide levels go up. This is called hypercarbia. There are several problems with this hypothesis: a) some symptoms of hypercarbia are similar to a near-death experience, but others are absolutely not; and b) carbon dioxide levels in the blood of patients under resuscitation are closely monitored. No ICU team would allow a significant buildup. In one study, whilst having an NDE, a patient even had a *lower than normal* concentration of CO_2 in his blood.

However, there is another, more fundamental issue undermining all these age-old explanations. Think carefully: why should people fantasise, project, hallucinate, experience symptoms of hypoxia or hypercarbia *when they have no functioning brain?*

Therefore, there remains one last line of defence for those who cannot accept that mind is somehow independent from the physical brain. They say it's a matter of *timing*. The experience happens *before the brain goes out*, or *after*, as the brain is recovering from the non-functioning state and consciousness is gradually restored. But here, again, we have several problems. First, at the onset, the loss of consciousness happens in a matter of milliseconds. One moment the person is fully conscious, and one instant later he or she is in a coma. How on earth can you have an experience you can talk about for days in those few milliseconds? Secondly, the recovery from the state of brain disruption happens through a state of confusion. As they come out of a coma, people are dazed, semi-conscious, disoriented. On the contrary, NDErs are hyper-conscious, completely lucid and very well oriented. Thirdly, you have to know that near death experiences are remembered in vivid details 15, 20, 25 years after the experience itself. According to the materialist model of mind, the formation of these long-term memories requires a fully functional brain, and requires time. How can this happen in the milliseconds before the coma, and during the period of recovery from total disruption?

A strong reason for hope

At the end of this long examination of the phenomenon, I hope I have convinced you that, even only based on the evidence from NDEs, a rational person can believe in an afterlife. Let me then sum up the whole meaning, significance and value of this most extraordinary human experience with the words of NDEr Craig, who in fact speaks for so many others who have had the experience and drew the same conclusions:

"1. There is nothing whatever to fear about death.

2. Dying is peaceful and beautiful.

3. Life does not begin with birth and does not end with death.

4. Life is precious – live it to the fullest.

5. The body and its senses are a tremendous gift – appreciate them.

6. What matters most in life is love.

7. Living a life oriented towards materialistic acquisition is missing the point.

8. Cooperation rather than competition makes for a better world.

9. Being a big success in life is not all it is cracked up to be.

10. Seeking knowledge is important – you take that with you."

Proof of Hell?

Before we leave the NDE subject, I feel compelled to touch on a somewhat difficult subject. I do this out of intellectual honesty, because since the beginning I have asked you to use your reason and critical faculties, rather than accepting what I say as a matter of faith, or just because it is comforting. Please always remember that the bulk of this book is dedicated to building the credibility of the sources we will use when, at the end, we will try to draw a "map" of the afterlife and describe what actually happens when we die.

So, my intellectual honesty compels me to tell you something that, if you are well informed on NDEs, you may already know: the hard, confusing reality is that not all NDEs are heavenly, pleasant, wondrous and uplifting. In fact, about 15% are not. Of those, most consist of a sense of emptiness, dullness, and between 1 and 2% are outright unpleasant and even harrowing. The really puzzling thing is that no correlation between the life history, beliefs, behaviour or attitudes of a person and the likelihood of having a radiant or harrowing NDE has been established.

Despite this lack of correlation, some, like cardiologist Dr Maurice Rawlings, go as far as saying that negative NDEs are proof of the existence of Hell (in the case of Dr Rawlings, going on to say that only conversion to conservative, biblically literal Christianity would save people from that!). Personally, I think that this is nonsense. As much nonsense, however, as assuming that positive NDEs are proof of Heaven.

NDEs, as we understand them today, are not "proof" of anything other than the fact that people have them. However, I am completely of the view shared by all foremost NDE researchers, who think that they are "strongly indicative" of survival of consciousness to bodily death.

Where does this leave us, then? Well, to begin with, it would appear that, as spirit communicators have been telling us consistently for centuries, we do not die. The body dies, but "we" go on living. This is very important, and should come as welcome news for most. Then, to try to make some sense of neutral or negative NDEs, I have to introduce a concept which is simple and complicated at the same time. That is – the idea is simple, but its application and the enormous effect it has on our experiences after we have shed our physical body may be difficult to grasp at first. This is a concept on which we will return in much greater details in later chapters, when we will be describing the "geography" of the afterlife.

The concept is this: as explained to us by countless voices from the Spirit world (I use "Spirit" for lack of a better word to describe the environment in which discarnate personalities appear to exist), the world our mind/consciousness/personality inhabits after the death of the physical body is literally created by our own thoughts. It feels completely real (most describe it as "more real than everyday physical reality"), and that includes the sensation, for many, of still having a physical body. Yet it is a world that "responds" to our thoughts. For example, spirit communicators often say that to move to a particular place it is enough to think of it, or to wish to be there, and instantaneously one finds himself/herself in that place. There's much more to this, and as I said we'll come back to it later. For the time being, think of the afterlife as a world largely shaped by our thoughts.

Back to NDEs, then, what is weird about the fact that a Christian will report having seen Jesus and a Hindu will tell about one of the many deities of that religion? Or a non-religious person will talk about a "being of light"? The underlying reality is the same, but our thoughts "shape" it so as to give us different experiences. And, what is weird about the fact that people who die suddenly are often said not to have realised that they have died, and remain for longer in what we'll describe as the "lower" levels of the Spirit world, in a reality that resembles closely their life on earth?

I therefore suspect that, in negative NDEs, something goes "wrong" with the thinking process. Confused by finding itself in an unexpected, non-physical environment, the mind picks on certain memories, thoughts or perhaps hidden beliefs or sense of guilt and creates an experience which is sometimes dull and, rarely, frankly harrowing, including images consistent with the Christian Hell.

Please reflect carefully on the following. The Buddhist tradition is very insistent that your state of mind at the moment of death will largely determine what comes immediately afterwards: prepare for death, think about death, try to have as a spiritually peaceful transition as possible, and your early experiences in the afterlife will be as joyous as the ones reported by the vast majority of NDErs. Interestingly, an old and almost forgotten prayer of the Christian tradition, going back to the Middle Ages says "God, please save me from a sudden death". The concept is the same: be prepared for the transition, expect to feel as alive as ever when your body will have stopped working. Finally, and crucially, this wisdom has been shared with us by the very people who have made that transition. Speaking to us though mediums and other channels, communicators from the Spirit world have time and again encouraged us to learn about the afterlife, to be prepared for and welcome the transition when the time comes. That will be our best guarantee to easily step into the world of Light that awaits all of us.

Chapter five

What deathbed visions are, and why we should trust them

This is the second chapter of "substance" in this book. Like the previous one, it is going to be rather long and packed with information. Once more, I recommend that you follow it with attention. On the one hand, its "hope generating" potential is very high, in itself. We will learn that, as we approach the transition we call death, many of us – most, actually – seem to be allowed to take a peek into the world that awaits us, and this is invariably a joyous experience. On the other, we have to do what we have done with NDEs: describe the phenomenon in some detail and critically examine possible alternative explanations. This work is important, because testimony from what we call Deathbed Visions (from now on, for brevity, DBVs) is also critical for our main aim of building a "roadmap" for the dying process and a "geography" of the afterlife.

Before we begin discussing DBVs, however, we have to take a preliminary step, and describe a phenomenon which is as well-known in the medical and caring professions as is – for a materialist worldview – utterly incredible. I want to tell you about the medical mystery called Terminal Lucidity.

The mystery of terminal lucidity

According to Wikipedia: "Terminal lucidity, rally before death or end-of-life rally, refers to an unexpected return of mental clarity and memory, or suddenly regained consciousness that occurs in the time shortly before death in patients suffering from severe psychiatric or neurological disorders. This phenomenon has been noted in patients with schizophrenia, tumors, strokes, meningitis, Parkinson's disease, and Alzheimer's disease". Instead of providing more definitions or descriptions, let me "bite the bullet" and give you a couple of accounts, reported by witnesses to Dr Alexander Batthyany, one of the foremost researchers in this field.

> "My grandfather was in palliative care for dementia. He had severe cognitive decline over the months preceding his death. There was no recognition of family or friends, paranoia, hallucinations, confusion, social withdrawal, refusal of food and drink, mumbling incoherent speech, and a lack of ability to toilet or shower himself. He awoke and began talking in a clear voice with obvious recognition of family and surroundings. He was able to inquire about family and friends that he had not been able to recognize previously. He asked that the books he had borrowed months ago be returned to their owner. He said he wished his death would come quicker. After 20 minutes, he became tired, fell asleep, and died shortly afterward."

> "She was her old self. Talkative, laughing, she thanked me for the card and plant that she seemed to not even recognize just days before. She requested a chocolate latte. She drank every drop. She reminisced about her sisters, her children, and grandchildren. For the first time in a long time, she seemed happy and not in pain."

Both these cases refer to patients with dementia, of which Alzheimer's disease is a common form. Anybody having had an experience – perhaps a loved one, a relative, a friend – with somebody suffering from dementia will have been shocked. Especially in the advanced stages, a person with dementia is not "there" anymore. Some seem to drift in a peaceful nothingness (no speech, no memory, no recognition of even the closest relatives – no mental life at all). Others, unfortunately, as in the first case above, appear to be going through Hell on earth. In any case, any health professional will tell you that advance dementia coincides with the disappearance of all mental faculties that make up "ourselves". Except, that is, in the cases of Terminal Lucidity, which are much more numerous than one may think.

These cases seem to be telling us that, as the physical brain of these patients is progressively ravaged by the disease, "they" are still there, with their entire awareness, personality, mannerism, memories, affections, experiences. You will have already noticed the striking similarity with NDEs: there, patients in a state of clinical death, with no functioning brain whatsoever, maintain all their mind faculties intact.

Is the physical brain actually *limiting* consciousness?

In order to make sense of these two large areas of evidence, we can only acknowledge, as I have said from the beginning of this book, that mind is related to, but independent from the electrical and chemical activity of a normal brain. This is admittedly a hard conclusion to draw, but we are compelled to it based on empirical evidence – based on *facts*, on what happens. And, if we accept this conclusion, then I would like to offer a very tentative explanation. Not a complete theory. Rather, just a simple explanation that suggest a mechanism and tries to account for what happens in NDEs and DBVs.

Imagine that, instead of being the source and origin of consciousness, the physical brain was just like a radio transmitter and receiver, technically called transceiver. Imagine that mind, consciousness, memory, personality exist outside the brain, just as a radio broadcast exists outside a radio device. Then, the brain would be an interface, a channel of communication between the physical world and this "field" of consciousness that we imagine exists outside it. The "transmitter" part of the brain would then, for example, transfer the experiences of the physical world we make through the senses and store them in the outside field as memories.

The "receiver" part would tune into this external field and make memories, thoughts, feelings available for use in the physical world. This would obviously be a very complex and finely tuned mechanism, one which would be easily disrupted by a condition like dementia. The signs shown by a dementia patient, then, would not mean that "he" or "she" have disappeared. Rather, they would indicate that the receiving and transmitting mechanism is not functioning as it should.

There is one last element of this tentative explanation that we have to consider. If we liken the physical brain to a radio transceiver, then we also have to imagine that it has a very narrow "filter". Just like the radio we have in the car has a filter that allows us to tune precisely into one station, without being disturbed by other stations on nearby frequencies, when it tunes into the external field of consciousness the "normal" brain filters out all that is not strictly and directly related to our experience of living in the physical world.

We have now all the ingredient to dare an explanation: with a mechanism that we do not understand, it seems that, as the body approaches death (in DBVs) or it is actually dead (in NDEs), this "filter" becomes much wider. We then become conscious of non-physical realities that have always been there, but were filtered out by the brain. In these special circumstances, we have a direct experience of our disembodied (or "discarnate", as it is often said in technical terms) consciousness. We do indeed have a taste of the afterlife, this spiritual dimension which is always inside and all around us, but which is normally hidden because of the limitations imposed by the brain. Essentially, I go back to the very core of my convictions: we are not bodies with a consciousness we lose at death. We are consciousness, with a body we lose at death. In the exceptional circumstances of DBVs and NDEs, we temporarily straddle the fine line between having and not having a body, but the consciousness remains intact.

Well, I hope I have not confused you too much. You may perhaps want to read the last few paragraphs again, and reflect a little bit on the model I (and a lot of people much more learned than me) tentatively propose. Then, we can dig deeper into the fascinating, wondrous phenomenon of Deathbed Visions.

The last 48 hours

In fact, we can consider DBVs as a "special case" of terminal lucidity. The general picture is the same: typically within 48 hours from the moment of death – and generally closer to it – people do show a sudden, marked, inexplicable improvement in their physical and mental situation. They liven up, they brighten up, often starting to talk in excited tones. What sets DBV apart from simple terminal lucidity is that these persons do not just talk or converse about anything – *they describe with extraordinary consistency what appear as visions of the afterlife*, as well as of deceased loved ones who are said to have come to facilitate the transition and "take them over". Often long, excited conversations take place between the person on the deathbed and these invisible (for other people in the room) visitors allegedly from the Spirit world.

In order to make the transition from the general subject of terminal lucidity to the specific case of DBVs, let me tell you about the case of a young German woman named Anna ("Käthe") Katharina Ehmer, who died in 1922. Her case is especially valuable, because it was witnessed by two highly respected and influential local figures: Wilhem Wittneben, the chief physician at what was then one of the largest insane asylums in Germany (Hephata), and Friedrich Happich, the director of that same institution. Over the years, both Wittneben and Happich relayed the experience many times in speeches and writings, and their independent descriptions of the incident cross-verified each other.

Käthe was among the most profoundly disabled of the patients at the asylum. Happich paints a vivid picture of her mental status. "From birth on," he writes, "she was seriously retarded. She had never learned to speak a single word. She stared for hours on a particular spot, then fidgeted for hours without a break. She gorged her food, fouled herself day and night, uttered an animal-like sound, and slept ... never [taking] notice of her environment even for a second." As if that weren't enough, Käthe suffered several severe meningitis infections over the years that had damaged her cortical brain tissue.

Yet, despite all this, as the woman lay dying (shortly after having her leg amputated from osseous tuberculosis—talk about bad luck), Wittneben, Happich, and other staff members at the facility gathered in astonishment at her bedside. "Käthe," wrote Happich, "who had never spoken a single word, being entirely mentally disabled from birth on, sang dying songs to herself. Specifically, she sang over and over again, 'Where does the soul find its home, its peace? Peace, peace, heavenly peace!' For half an hour she sang. Her face, up to then so stultified, was transfigured and spiritualized. Then, she quietly passed away."

You may think that, since I quoted a case from a century ago, that such cases are rare and exceptional. Nothing could be further from the truth. They are so common, in fact, that they are well known by anybody working in hospices and palliative care centres, as well as in general hospital wards. The phenomenon is so widespread that many universities include it as a subject of study in their nursing degrees, to prepare future nurses to deal with something they are very likely to encounter in their practice and requires delicate handling, both for the person having the visions and for any loved one who may be in attendance. A few years ago, as I was doing research for another book, I came across a discussion board on allnurses.com, a community website dedicated to sharing information among registered nurses. I searched for the term "deathbed visions" and I was astonished to find 121 pages of discussion! Literally thousands of posts in which these health professionals talk about the experiences they had assisting people at the moment of their death, all describing and commenting on the same kind of phenomenon.

Important research data

Right, you may say, DBV are frequent, but exactly how frequent? In the 1970s, Prof Erlendur Harldsson of the University of Iceland and Karlis Osis PhD, then director of research at the American Society for Psychical Research, carried out an extensive, systematic study. They began by contacting hospital wards where many people died. They met with doctors and nursing staff and distributed a questionnaire, to learn whether they had observed hallucinations in dying patients, and their content, and if the patients had mentioned people or described heavenly surroundings. They also asked about experiences of patients who had lost consciousness, almost died, and returned back to life. They inquired about incidents where the emotional well-being of patients improved markedly just before dying. Healthcare workers who had observed such cases, were singled out for a thorough interview. In all, 435 doctors and nursing staff were interviewed in India and 442 in the US.

The first conclusion of this study is almost stunning: about ten percent of people are conscious at the moment of their death; of them, *two thirds have deathbed visions!* This is indeed an extraordinary number – no surprise that the phenomenon is so well known by those who assist the dying. The study I mentioned – and several others which followed – reveal other interesting features of this phenomenon, and, like it was the case for NDEs, show that all the "normal" explanations that have been proposed over the years do not account for the facts. Before discussing this further, however, let's look at the account by a medical doctor, to fully appreciate the wonderful human dimension of DBVs.

> "When I went into oncology, it never occurred to me that I might see one of my loved ones terminally ill. So when I got the news that my younger brother, Mike, who was just 41, had cancer, it was really hard for me to act as a doctor and not a saddened man who was afraid to lose his brother.
>
> Mike was just hitting his stride; he enjoyed his career and was seeing a lot of success in his real-estate

investments. It seemed incomprehensible that his cancer was advanced, and it was almost impossible for my family to face the reality that it may be too late. I tried to remain hopeful. But I knew too much.

One day near the end, my mother and I were sitting with Mike, who was quiet but not sleeping. Then he suddenly started talking, as if there was someone standing right in front of him (he definitely wasn't addressing my mom or me). Mom and I looked at each other in a way that said, 'What is this?'

We soon realised that Mike was indeed talking to someone, and as we listened to the conversation, it dawned on us that he was speaking to my father's parents. He had been very close to them and loved them both very much. When Grandma died, Mike started spending more time with our grandfather. Since my cousins and I were away at school, we were grateful that my brother was there and could visit him so often. After Grandpa died, it hit Mike very hard. So the notion that it was my grandparents who came to my brother as he was dying wasn't that surprising.

As a doctor, it's very easy to dismiss this sort of thing until you see it first-hand. Could my brother's vision have been a dream state? Was it a result of oxygen deprivation? A side effects of the medications? All were possible, but for my mother and I none of those options felt right. It felt profound. Real. Neither one of us wanted to interfere, so we just observed.

For the next few hours, mom and I watched Mike on and off the conversation. We could never quite make out exactly what he was saying, but we could hear him call both of my grandparents by name. He also had a tender, sweet look on his face. Of all the things that we were doing to him – from end-of-life care to making sure that he got the best of everything – this 'visit' seemed to bring him the most comfort.

Before this episode, there was a sense of tension and struggle in the air, but now there seemed to be only peace surrounding my brother. I truly believe that it was a result of my grandparents' visit as he died.

One family member asked me, 'As a doctor, what do you make of this?' And I responded, 'I don't make anything of it as a doctor. I don't have a scientific explanation. I only have my *own* experience to draw from. I took it at face value and knew it was an authentic part of the process.'

When my patients have similar experiences, I don't question it as a doctor. I just accept that this is what's going on. If it feels real to a patient, so be it. But this is definitely not the kind of thing that they teach in medical school."

Wonderful, isn't it? But yet, we are left with many of the same questions we had when we started examining NDEs. Essentially, are these experiences "real"? Here, as we have done before, I must ask you to become a bit of a "CSI" investigator – like in the popular TV series – and look at this phenomenon from all possible angles.

Are DBVs for real?

Is it not possible, for example, that, coming close to the moment of death, people would simply have hallucinations? This is in fact the first "explanation" brought up by those who cannot bring themselves to accept the reality of an afterlife. Well, research rules out this hypothesis as:

1) Compared to the hallucinations produced by a sick brain, the typical deathbed vision is shorter in duration, is more coherent and much more related to the situation of the patient.

2) Unlike what happens in hallucinations, the patient is logical and well oriented. He or she insists that he or she is seeing something real.

3) The majority of the apparitions are of deceased people. This hardly ever happens in hallucinations.

4) 83% of dying people see apparitions of dead relatives. The mentally ill conjure up strange, bizarre characters.

5) Hallucinations are generally stressful. Instead, the predominant reaction of patients who see apparitions is of serenity and peace.

OK, then – DBVs are not hallucinations. Would it instead be possible that they are related to medical factors, so important near the moment of death. Here again, research has some clear answers:

1) There is no correlation between patients taking drugs like morphine and the frequency of deathbed visions.

2) Brain disturbances caused by disease, injury or uremic poisoning actually decrease the frequency of apparitions.

3) A medical history of hallucinations does not increase the frequency of apparitions.

Furthermore a most interesting, intriguing finding of research is there appear to be no correlation between the patients' religious beliefs, or any expectation about the afterlife, and the frequency or content of DBVs. The study carried out in the US and India showed that:

1) Christian American patients often report visions of Heaven, but Hell and devils are almost never mentioned. Christian ideas of judgment, salvation and redemption are totally absent.

2) In India, basic Hindu beliefs like reincarnation and dissolution in Brahma were never mentioned.

3) Eleven core phenomena suggestive of an afterlife were found to be common to both Indian and American deathbed visions.

4) Similarities outweigh the differences by a large margin, indicating a universal human experience rather than one produced by culture.

Finally, and most importantly, psychological factors do not have an influence either. First of all, stress levels do not affect how often people have DBVs. Secondly, apparitions are clearly not wish fulfilment:

1) The desire to see somebody does not affect the frequency of apparitions.

2) Patients do not automatically see people they specifically wanted to see.

And, I kept this for last because really these are two fundamentally important pieces of evidence -

3) Patients who expect to die, but make a recovery *do not have DBVs*. At the same time, patients who expect to live but end up dying *do have DBVs!* Do you remember what we said about NDEs? That the closer a patient comes to actually dying – that is, crossing the threshold with no return – the higher the likelihood to have NDEs? Here we have a very similar situation, one in which it is the *proximity to actual death* that triggers the phenomenon, and not just the expectation. Earlier in the chapter we compared the physical brain to a radio transceiver with a narrow filter that, under normal circumstances, only allows us to interact with the physical world. This kind of theory would apply very well to DBVs: coming close to actually crossing the threshold, the radio's filter becomes wider, and we seem to be allowed to take a look into and interact with the spiritual, nonphysical dimension that awaits us.

4) Unbelievably – and this, for me, is the true nail in the coffin of any materialist explanation – there is a vast literature of well researched cases in which people having DBVs see dead relatives *they didn't know were dead at the moment the vision took place*. In the

chapter on what happens preceding the moment of death we will look at several of these instances. For now, the following case, from the *Proceedings* of the Society for Psychical Research (SPR), should give you a good introduction, as it illustrates this extraordinary phenomenon quite well (names have been changed to protect the original identities).

> "Some sixteen years ago, one day Mrs Jones said to me, 'We have some people staying here all next week. Do you know any person I could get to sing with the girls?' I suggested that an acquaintance of mine, Mr Fox, had a daughter with a fine voice, who was training as a public singer, and I would write to him and ask if he would allow her to come down and spend a week with us. On my wife's approval I wrote and Miss Fox came down for a week, and then left. As far as I know, Mrs Jones never saw her again. Shortly after, I called on Mr Fox, thanked him for allowing his daughter to come to us, and said we were all much pleased with her. Mr Fox replied, 'I fear you have spoilt her, for she says she never passed such a happy week in her life.' Miss Fox did not come out as a singer, but shortly after Mr Brown and none of us saw her again.
>
> Six or seven years passed and Mrs Jones, who had been long ill, was dying, in fact she did die the following day. I was sitting at the foot of her bed talking over some business matters that she was anxious to arrange, being perfectly composed and in thorough possession of her senses. She changed the subject and said, 'Do you hear those voices singing?' I replied that I did not and she said, 'I have heard them several times today and I am sure they are the angels welcoming me to Heaven'; but, she added, 'It is strange there is a voice amongst them I am sure I know, and I cannot remember whose voice it is.' Suddenly, she stopped and said, pointing straight over my head, 'Why, there she is in the corner of the room; it is Julia Fox; she is coming on; she is leaning over you; she has her hands up, she is praying; do look, she is

going.' I turned but could not see nothing. Mrs Jones then said, 'She is gone.' All these things I imagined to be the fantasies of a dying person.

Two days afterwards, taking up the *Times* newspaper, I saw recorded the death of Julia Fox, wife of Mr Brown. I was so astounded that in a day or so after the funeral, I asked Mr Fox if Julia, his daughter, was dead. He said, 'Yes, poor thing, she died of puerperal fever. On the day she died she began singing in the morning and sung until she died.'"

The SPR researchers who investigated the case add:

"Julia Fox died on February 2nd at six or thereabout in the morning. Mrs Jones died on February 13, at about four in the evening. The announce of the death of Mrs Fox did not come out until February 14. All witnesses we interviewed agree that Mrs Jones was never subject to hallucinations of any sort."

Shared Death Experiences

To end this chapter, we still have to briefly look at one – if possible – even more astounding phenomenon: Shared Death Experiences, which as usual we will refer to with the acronym SDEs.

If you look at most of the descriptions of DBVs, they are provided by witnesses (a nurse, a doctor, a relative) who happen to be present when the dying person has the experience. Typically, the witness (often more than one) describes the behaviour of the dying person – strongly suggesting he or she is interacting with an alternative reality *which the witness cannot see*. In the same manner, NDErs recount an experience that *they* have had – a private, very vivid conscious experience at a moment when they have no functioning brain.

Instead, and this is a dramatic difference, in SDEs witnesses *do take part* in this incredible, spiritually transformative experience at the moment of one person's "death".

SDEs have been documented in research by the Society for Psychical Research in London since the late 1800s. Peter Fenwick, MD, and Elizabeth Fenwick, RN, who research end-of-life phenomena, have collected hundreds of SDE accounts in the United Kingdom and in Northern Europe. Dr Raymond Moody formally coined the term "Shared Death Experience" in his 2009 book, Glimpses of Eternity.

The core elements of the SDE are remarkably similar to those of the NDE, but may also contain some elements of the DBV. The following elements may characterize Shared Death Experiences:

- Mist at death
- Hearing beautiful music
- Change in the geometry of the room
- Strong Upward Pull on the Body
- Shared Out-of-Body Experience
- Seeing a Mystical Light
- Empathically Co-living the Life Review of the Dying Person
- Greeted by Beings of Light
- Encountering Heavenly Realms
- Boundary in the Heavenly Realm

Just as we have seen in NDEs, those who have an SDE show remarkable, strongly transformative psychological and behavioural changes, including: dramatic grief reduction, knowing that the one who has died is actually alive and well in the afterlife; greatly reduced fear and apprehension of death; increased belief in an afterlife; a deeper understanding and refocusing on one's purpose in this life.

To conclude this quick review of SDEs, let me quote Dr Raymond Moody himself, as he discusses some differences between NDEs and SDEs.

> I studied shared-death experiences just as I had done with near-death experiences nearly four decades earlier, dissecting them into their elements. The shared-death experiences contained most of the traditional elements of the near-death experience, including tunnel experiences, seeing a bright mystical light, out-of-body experiences, even the transformational quality found in near-death experiencers. But there were four differences that I found to be extraordinary and new.
>
> Mystical Music: Those who have shared-death experiences very often hear music emanating from the surroundings. It is common for the music to be heard by several people, even those coming and going, and it can frequently last for long periods of time. The people I surveyed described this music in various ways. To some it was "the most beautiful and intricate music I have ever heard," while to others it was "the soft, wild notes of an Aeolian harp." This phenomenon was also reported in the nineteenth-century work of researchers Gurney, Myers, and Podmore. There is no known explanation, other than to call it "the music of the spheres."
>
> Geometric Changes in the Environment: Even though my family experienced this change in geometry when my mother died, it is still difficult for me to describe it, and the people I spoke to who had had the same experience were no better able to find words for it. A woman I interviewed said simply that the square room "shifted." A man who'd had a shared-death experience at the bedside of his mother offered a confusing description of a room that "collapsed and expanded at the same time. It was as though I was witnessing an alternative geometry." Others said that the room opened

into an "alternative reality" where "time is not a factor." And still another person likened this change in geometry to Disneyland, in that "it made me realize that most of the stuff that happens in the world happens behind the scenes and that all we see is the surface, where the functioning part is."

I don't know what this change in geometry really means. From my personal experience and the descriptions of others, it seems as though people who are dying, and sometimes those around them, are led to a different dimension.

A Shared Mystical Light: The most profoundly transformative part of a near-death experience is the encounter with a mystical light. Those who see the light never forget it. Sometimes these individuals feel the light, as though it is palpable. Many NDEers declare that the light emits purity, love, and peace.

Those who have had shared-death experiences say the same thing. Individuals and groups have said that the room of a dying loved one "filled up" with light. Some describe this as "a light that is like being swept up into a cloud." I have heard it described as "a light that is vivid and bright, but not in the way that we see with our eyes." Other descriptors have been "translucent," "a light filled with love," "a light that tickled me," and a "long-lasting light that stays even when it's gone."

An experience of light shared by a number of people at a deathbed does a lot to demolish the sceptics' argument that the light seen by those who have near-death experiences is nothing more than the dying brain shorting out. If a number of people who are not ill or dying share a mystical experience of light, then the light can't be caused by the dying brain of just one of them.

Mystical Experience: Another common event in the shared-death experience is seeing emissions of mist from the dying. This mist is described as "white smoke," steam, fog, and so on. Often it takes on a human shape.

I have spoken to many doctors, nurses, and hospice workers who have seen this mist. One doctor in Georgia who saw it happen twice within six months said simply, "A mist formed over the chest area and hovered there." A hospice worker in North Carolina twice saw mist rising from a dying patient and described what she saw as clouds with "a sort of mist that forms around the head or chest. There seems to be some kind of electricity to it, like an electrical disturbance."

I don't know how to interpret the mist that some see at the point of death. There are so many who see it that it makes no sense to me to say that death is playing tricks on the eyes or that these are hallucinations. Plus, this is by far the most common element reported by those who have shared-death experiences.

Chapter six

Who are spirit communicators, and why is it reasonable to trust them?

An extraordinary night of mediumship

The Pavilion theatre in Glasgow is one of the oldest in Scotland, but it has gone through various stages of modernisation, and tonight, as my wife and I take our seats in the second row of the gallery, it looks like it could be a performance venue in Las Vegas. The place is not very big, it probably holds some 500 people in the stalls and another 200 in the single gallery, but tonight there practically is not one seat free. For years Glaswegians have flocked to the increasingly rare public performances of Gordon Smith, the *psychic barber*, hailed as one of the most formidable mediums active in the UK today.

I have been following Gordon for quite some time, since I learned about his participation as one of the research mediums in the PRISM (Psychical Research Involving Selected Mediums) programme run at Glasgow University by Professor Emeritus Archie Roy and fellow physicist Trisha Robertson in the early 1990s. He is a pretty unique character. The seventh son of a seventh son (tradition would have it that this is a predictor of special powers), Gordon grew up in a deprived, violent area of the city, with the added difficulty of being gay – definitely not an asset in the macho-dominated gang culture of the area.

Despite all that, he turned out to be the most adorable, personable, caring person you could think of. His gift for mediumship, as it often is the case with such rare birds, started showing up early in life, but it was only as a young adult that, whilst running his famous barber shop, Gordon got into serious development work, training amongst others with celebrity medium Alfred Best, who took him on almost as a child prodigy. Soon enough, Gordon was performing at services in Spiritualist churches all around Scotland, hailed by the Daily Mail newspaper "Britain's most accurate medium".

I had seen, and studied in depth, a number of video recordings of Gordon Smith's public performances and private séances (note that Gordon *never* charges money for sitting privately with bereaved people). I was mesmerised. The quantity and quality of the information he manages to convey about deceased people he could not possibly know anything about is simply stunning. So, both my wife and I are expecting great things from tonight's stage performance.

The format is simple. Gordon, alone on stage, delivers a weird mix between hair-raisingly accurate information about deceased people, often moving their surviving loved ones to tears, and what you would describe almost as stand-up comedy in the characteristic Glasgow patter. He manages to be serious, dramatic and most compassionate in his readings, and still have a light heart and lift the general atmosphere with rapid-fire, humorous remarks.

The bottom line is that, reading after reading, names, places, ages, modes of death, family details down to the most apparently mundane (but exceedingly meaningful for the bereaved persons) keep coming from this man in his early fifties, who paces the stage, delivering a steady flow of information without interruption.

Then, at some point, he moves towards the left of the stage, and pauses, as if concentrating. And he goes, "I have a young man here. Somebody who died a violent death. He tells me that it was not his fault, though. He happened to find himself at the wrong place at the wrong time. Does this mean anything to anybody?" A woman in the third or fourth row of the stalls, almost directly opposite where

Gordon had moved on stage, raises her hand and says that, yes, she could possibly know who this person is. Gordon then provides a date of when the accident happened, which is confirmed by the lady, and then quite precisely the area of town where it happened. At that stage the lady is "sold", and starts being emotional. Gordon then continues, "This young man tells me that the police investigation is still open. No justice has been done yet." Further confirmation from the lady. Gordon again, "He tells me that his Mum was badly affected by the events, to the point that she was recently admitted to a psychiatry ward." To which the woman answers, "Absolutely. I have been visiting her in hospital just yesterday!"

That is the moment when a blonde woman in her thirties stands up, two seats to our left, and shouts down towards the stage, "Gordon! 'At's ma wee brother yer talkin' aboot!"

The crucial question

So, in short, *this* is mediumship. I wanted to tell this real-life episode of 2016 because it happened to *me. I* was there. I witnessed, for almost two hours, an extraordinary display of an extraordinary – and totally inexplicable, if you take a materialist view – ability. Gordon Smith is a medium, and as such the only thing he does is *talk to the dead*, for the sole benefit of their bereaved loved ones. No predicting the future, no juicy details about one's next lover, no psychic career advice.

I was there, at the Pavilion theatre, and things happened exactly as I had seen in the recorded videos. Gordon walks into a place packed with hundreds of people, and pulls out of a mysterious hat the most incredibly detailed information. And, in a "live" situation, the same questions filled my mind as they did when I was watching the videos. Is there a *normal* explanation for what I am seeing? I try to figure out an exceedingly complicated scam system by which he would, way ahead of the performance, make agreements with at least a couple dozen people, make sure they are distributed evenly in the theatre, then, on the night of the performance, deliver fake stories on stage which his "accomplices" would recognise, often to the point of breaking down in tears (they and, often, those who have come with them to the show).

Such would be a very complicated organisation, difficult to set up – one in which plenty can go wrong. And doing this for years, all over the world, without a single hitch, without *ever* anybody raising the slightest doubt? And for what reason? Money? He doesn't charge much for these public performances – imagine if he had to pay 20 or 30 accomplices. And how would I explain the same accuracy and breadth of information that he produces in private sittings, and when performing at Spiritualist churches (as I said, without charging any money)? Tons of questions, which always remain without an answer. Unless, that is, I and we all accept that Gordon, like all gifted mediums, *really do talk to the dead*.

This is truly a crucial question, for the discarnates speaking to us through mediums are the third major source of information that I will use in my attempt to explain to you what happens when we die and what the spirit world may look like. As it was the case for Near-Death Experiences and Deathbed Visions, we have to carry out a sort of "detective work" to make sure as best we can that the witnesses we will use are indeed who they claim to be: persons who once lived on earth and who go on living in a nonmaterial dimension, where they retain their mind, thoughts, personality, memories and affections.

Different kinds of mediumship

I hope you will remember what I said in an earlier chapter concerning the physical brain possibly acting as a "filter" and blocking out anything that is not directly connected with our life in the physical world. You will remember that I also said that said "filter" function appears to weaken when we approach death, so that NDErs and people having DBVs are allowed to perceive a much broader, nonphysical reality, including the world that awaits us after death. If we accept this explanation – which is not a theory but simply a way to try to make sense of the facts, then the persons we call mediums are born with a "wider filter" than any of us, and have various levels of perceptions of such nonmaterial realms. Before we go any further, we need to clarify a couple of key points.

First, although it can be developed to some extent, and although in some cases the gift of mediumship becomes apparent only in later life, it seems that mediums are born with such a "wider filter". Albert Best, one of the greatest of all time, famously said, "You can learn mediumship as much as you can learn to have blue eyes".

Secondly, like all human talents, this gift is rare and very unevenly distributed. There is a select group whom I would call "stars" (at any given time during the last two centuries, two or three dozen individuals at best around the world). Then there is a much larger group which I would describe as "glowbugs". These are the hundreds, possibly thousands of working mediums, providing evidence of survival in Spiritualist churches and – especially in the US – in a thriving market of private sittings. As glowbugs, they still shine, but their luminosity is incomparably lower than that of the stars. The amount, specificity, accuracy and level of detail they provide about deceased loved ones is still enough for the bereaved to be able to recognise them with certainty, but we are far from the eye-popping performances of the stars. Finally, there are masses of people who call themselves mediums (out of self-delusion or because they are dishonest confidence tricksters), and who simply are not – they don't have any gift.

Nowadays, mediumship appears mostly (but by no means exclusively) confined to the modality we define as *mental mediumship*. This is what I briefly described in the case of the public (and private) readings of Gordon Smith: the medium remains conscious and appears to interact with the sitter (the person the reading is intended for) on one side and with one or more communicators on the spirit side. In the past, a frequent modality was the one of *trance mediumship*. In that case, the medium goes into an altered state of consciousness and is not aware of what goes on during the séance. Spirit communicators then in a way "take possession" of the body of the medium, and speak directly to the people the messages are intended to.

The literature on trance mediumship is exceedingly vast, and it is interesting to note that in practically all cases the communicators speak to the sitters with a voice that is easily recognised as their own, and different from the one of the medium, with inflections, mannerisms and vocabulary typical of when they were in the physical world. Similarly out of fashion – for reasons which we are unaware of – is mediumship through *automatic writing*. Here too, the spirit communicator takes some form of control of the body of the medium, who proceeds to writing messages (tens of pages, in certain cases) independently of their will. And, here too, the literature is enormous, with well researched tales, for instance, of mediums entertaining a normal conversation with a third person whilst writing messages from the spirit world at great speed.

An altogether different form of mediumship – a real challenge for our capacity of accepting, if not understanding – is *physical mediumship*. This too is a phenomenon that seemed to be more frequent in the past, but I am aware of several mediums and mediumship circles in different parts of the world where physical phenomena happen today, often under the most stringent scrutiny and control. What we define as physical phenomena include the movement of objects (such as table levitation), a variety of light phenomena and, especially, *direct voices*. These are the voices of the spirit communicators, which are heard distinctly, recognisably and seem to originate not from the medium, but essentially *out of thin air*, in different parts of the séance room. Physical mediumship, which includes macroscopic phenomena even more incredible than the ones I briefly mentioned, is, as I said, quite a challenge for all of us – researchers, scholars and the interested public. I have written extensively about it, and I consider it a bit of "specialist subject", generally beyond the scope of this book, which is dedicated to those who are facing the prospect of death.

The remainder of the chapter, as we did previously, will therefore be devoted to establishing the credibility of both the mediumship process and of the personalities who communicate with us through mediums, for they are our third main source of information on the process of dying and the afterlife.

Is it all a fraud?

Mediumship existed as long as mankind itself. However, it is fair to say that in its "modern" modality (one in which the mediums are essentially normal people, and not, like in the past, shamans, oracles, or other mystical/religious figures), it broke into the general public awareness in the mid-1800s, with the famous case of the Fox sisters in the US. Immediately, as news of the formidable feats of these modern mediums spread around the world, scores of self-appointed sceptics set out to try to "debunk", or explain away the alleged phenomena. For over 150 years, the so called "explanations" have been the same. They are limited in number – three, or four if we add a sophisticated and rarely used one, and denote first and foremost the ignorance of said sceptics about the phenomenon itself. I think it is useful, in our investigation, to use these "explanations" as a basis: we will "debunk the debunkers" with facts, and therefore hopefully establish the credibility of mediums and spirit communicators.

The first explanation immediately put forward when faced with something as preposterous as after-death communication is fraud. This is laughable for a number of reasons.

To begin with, sceptics want us to believe that mediums engage in fraud to acquire fame and wealth. Whilst it is true that there are plenty of confidence tricksters who prey on needy bereaved people to dishonestly earn some money, we have already said that they are *not* mediums. It is also true that *a few* real, gifted mediums do acquire considerable fame (think, for instance, of the *Long Island medium* we see on television), and *some*, particularly in the US, manage to make a pretty decent living through charging for private sittings. However, large numbers of mediums, including some in the category I defined as *stars,* acquire neither fame nor wealth. Gordon Smith, for instance, despite being well known in the UK, continued up until recently to make his living from his barber shop in Glasgow. Other *stars* are even actively shy and reserved, and perform their extraordinary feats in closed circles, far from the general public's eye and without ever charging a penny.

Furthermore, the hypothesis of fraud becomes untenable when you look at the quantity and quality of the information, and the circumstances under which it is provided. A discussion on this subject may take an entire book – or at least a long chapter – by itself, so let me just cite one example I described in my first book, *21 Days into the Afterlife*. This alone, I believe, will put the issue of fraud to rest.

This is the story of another very gifted but perhaps less known physical medium, John Sloan, and the researcher who thoroughly investigated him, Arthur Findlay. John Sloan was another Glasgow native, a packer in a warehouse, and a small shopkeeper. His relative lack of notoriety is probably due to his persistent refusal to become a public medium, to take money for his work, or to give demonstrations. Sloan himself had little interest for mediumship, and conducted sittings solely for the benefit of others. Arthur Findlay describes him as "an upright, good, honest man, with little learning, poor memory, and … average intelligence".

To have the medium at the disposal of the British College of Psychic Science, at some stage Hewat McKenzie found employment for Sloan in a London garage and made him accessible to various experimenters. After his return to Glasgow, he was experimented with for five years by Arthur Findlay, a successful stockbroker, a Justice of the Peace and the founder of the Glasgow Society for Psychical Research. In 1924 he published a small book on his findings: *An Investigation of Psychic Phenomena* with a preface by Sir William Barrett. This was followed by a larger volume: *On the Edge of the Etheric*, in 1931.

What makes Findlay's investigation of John Sloan particularly interesting is that he provides verbatim accounts of 24 séances held between April 1942 and July 1945, taken down by an expert stenographer, Miss Jean Darie. The séances in question, attended by between seven and eleven sitters each, were all held in Glasgow at the homes of various of the sitters, and never in Sloan's own home. Findlay went as far as sending copies of the verbatim transcripts to seven of the regular sitters and obtained signed statements that the accounts agreed with their own notes taken at the time.

Now, back to the issue of fraud. First, let's consider that Sloan held regular séances for over 50 years, usually in other people's homes and in front of many reliable witnesses, without any charge of trickery ever being made against him. Secondly, let's see what Findlay had to say on what would have been necessary if trickery were to have taken place.

1. Sloan would have had to engage an investigator to help him think up a new script for each sitting that reflected the many sitters who, at different times, regularly attended his séances over some 50 years, and a knowledge of such details of any dead friends and relatives who might communicate. Such knowledge would have had to include pet names used within families, together with other details of intricate family relationships.

2. The scripts would also have had to include appropriate material for many hundreds of other sitters who came as guests of the regular circle members, many of whom protected their anonymity before and during the sitting and yet still received satisfactory communications.

3. Accomplices would have been needed for each sitting in order to impersonate, from different positions in the room, the 40 or so characters who appeared in the script for each sitting and spoke through the independent voice method.

4. The accomplices would have had to be smuggled into the various private houses where the sittings were held, bringing with them any necessary props. In addition to using their voices, they would have had to keep two trumpets flying around the room, frequently at a great speed, and even touching the ceiling and beating on it, ring bells, and make small lights dance so expertly here and there that they were never caught by the sitters.

5. The accomplices would have had to manage all this in the dark, and in small rooms where most of the space was taken up by sitters, and without bumping into the sitters or into each other.

6. In addition, the accomplices would have had to find sitters unerringly in the dark in order to touch them – often on request – and to stroke and caress their faces.

7. Finally, the accomplices would have had to escape undetected from the room before the electric lights were switched on at the end of the sitting

So, what are we left with? 50 years of séances for neither money nor fame, thousands of sitters, top qualified investigators, strict controls, and never one accusation of fraud or trickery, on the one hand. On the other, an alleged system of fraud and accomplices so absurdly complicated to utterly defy common sense. Conclusion: fraud is very tempting as an explanation – it is simple and applies well to dishonest "non-mediums". For real mediumship, as demonstrated by Sloan's and hundreds of other extremely well investigated cases, it simply is a non-starter.

Is the medium "cold reading" the sitter?

The second explanation, typically put forward immediately after the first one, is that the medium engages in what is technically called "cold reading". Essentially, he or she will make a rather general statement – something like "I have a gentleman in spirit who wants to come across" – and carefully observes the reaction of the sitter, paying particular attention to nonverbal clues like facial expression, body movements and the like. Based on these, the sceptics say, the medium can tell whether he or she is going in the right direction, and progressively refine (or correct) the statements until something meaningful is produced. For instance, if the sitter gave signs of reacting positively to the statement "I have a gentleman", the medium can go on and try "It's an older gentleman, I get the feeling of a father figure…" etc. Essentially, cold reading is a subtle game of trial and error. Paired with the sitter's desire to believe, the sceptics say, it is a very powerful technique and can explain mediumship.

This, again, looks attractive. It's a simple explanation, for starters, and we all like simple explanations. Plus, it introduces a component of skill – the medium must be skilled in order to apply the technique effectively, and this explains why certain mediums are better than others. But, is it true?

Well, start by thinking of the short story I told you at the beginning of the chapter. Could Gordon Smith apply cold reading techniques with random members of a 500-strong audience? No, he obviously could not. The only possible explanation in cases of public demonstrations involving dozens or hundreds of people at a time is fraud, and we have already seen that fraud is very, very unlikely.

Then, you must know that, repeatedly, sceptics who consider themselves skilled in the "art" of cold reading have challenged mediums publicly. The format of the challenge – which I have seen on daytime TV several times – is simple: there are a few sitters, the sceptic and a medium. First, each sitter is "read" by the sceptic using cold reading techniques. Then, the same sitters are read by the medium, allegedly using his or her mediumship gift. The result, invariably, is that the medium wins hands down. Sitters consistently report more accuracy, more specificity, more information as such for the readings by the medium, whilst they rate the readings by the sceptic very general and they say that the sceptic was constantly "fishing" for information.

Lastly, there is one scientific method that definitely invalidates the "cold reading" hypothesis. It is the oldest – and the most effective – trick in the book of the psychical investigators, used already in the late 1800s. The fact that method is so well-known by the specialists and it has been so widely applied for some 150 years also demonstrates the basic, essential ignorance – or intellectual dishonesty – of the so-called sceptics. The method is called *proxy sitting*.

A proxy sitting is one in which the person who sits with the medium is *not* the person the reading is intended for. In the best protocols, this proxy sitter doesn't even know the intended sitter. There is *physically, practically* no possibility for the medium to "fish" or "cold read".

Let me explain with a concrete example. Let's say that Mary has lost her father, whose name was John, born, say, in 1937. Mary wants to hear from her father through a medium. Following the proxy sitting method, it is not Mary herself, but a third person, Margaret, who goes to see the medium. Margaret doesn't know Mary, let alone her deceased father. She is just told a name, John, and a date of birth, 1937. Margaret then goes to sit with the medium and gives John's name and date of birth. During the sitting, Margaret records in writing the content of the medium's reading in the greatest possible details. Finally, the reading recorded by Margaret is shown to Mary, who either confirms it as relevant and accurate or not.

The method works, consistently and spectacularly well, as I said already since the end of the 19th century. In particular, starting from the 1920's, we have published verbatim transcripts of literally thousands of proxy sitting experiments. An analysis of the statements by the mediums show that these are just as accurate and relevant as the ones provided in a normal setting, when the intended sitter is present. Professor Dodds, the rationalist President of the Society for Psychical Research from 1961-63, supervised a series of proxy sitting tests with the medium Nea Walker and was much impressed. He concluded, "The hypothesis of fraud, rational inference from disclosed facts, telepathy from the actual sitter, and co-incidence cannot either singly or in combination account for the results obtained."

A real-life proxy sitting, as it happened

Now, before going further, I feel that I need to give you, the reader, some further "meat" – some real-life examples drawn from the research literature, to make sure you fully appreciate what we are talking about. Let's therefore look at one of the verbatim transcripts I told you about.

Particularly well-known in the specialist circles is the investigation of superstar medium Gladys Leonard by noted psychical researcher Charles Drayton Thomas in the 1930s and 1940s. In 1932, Rev Thomas – a Methodist minister – carried out a number of sittings with Mrs Leonard as a proxy sitter for a couple of bereaved parents who had lost a child to diphtheria. In the course of eleven sittings, he was aided by an expert stenographer, who wrote down what the medium said, word by word. Here follows a selection of the 141 statements made by the medium (in italic), followed by the comments provided by the child's parents.

This boy had a pain in his hand (Bobbie sometimes lost the use of his right hand, and although he did not complain of pain he could not write while the condition lasted)

His glands were affected by a disease (the glands are affected in diphtheria)

The boy's neck and throat were affected (diphtheria principally affects the neck and throat)

He was very pleased at winning something not very long before he passed (nine weeks before he died, Bobbie had won a competition with a salt sifter shaped like a dog, of which he was very proud)

He played with something with numbers on... curved lines... grooves... and numbers... evenings after tea (Bobbie was particularly successful with a machine at a local fair which rewarded him with money for shooting into numbered circles; he played the game several times in the evenings after tea)

...a photograph of Bobbie... full faced... with something in front of him... a board in front of him... like at the back of a board or a tray... (the last photograph of Bobbie ever taken was of him in fancy dress as the knave of hearts, with boards in front and behind him representing cards)

...something has been given... a joke... wearing on his head... something round... new... just like a ring... no peak at all... (the knave of hearts

costume had a round crown, which Bobbie was so proud of putting on that his mother stopped him for fear of wearing it out)

His nose hurt (Bobbie was learning to box and his instructor gave him a blow on his nose that hurt; he had written in his diary "The instructor burst my nose")

Bobbie did some funny things for a boy... pulling something from the wall... thick string or rope... the pulling out seemed important... drawing it out as far as possible, and the letting it go back into the wall... something he seemed to do quite regularly (in the attic Bobbie had an arrangement for strengthening his muscles that consisted of a thin rope that ran through a pulley fixed to the wall and was attached to a heavy weight; pulling the rope from the wall raised the weight; Bobbie exercised with it rather regularly)

Lying on the floor... flat on the floor or something... sort of squirming about... hands and feet going (a correct reference to exercises Bobbie's boxing instructor gave him, and which he did in the attic – raising legs while on his back etc.)

OK – I think you get the idea by now: phenomenally detailed and precise statements about a boy the medium knew nothing about, given not to the boy's parents but to Rev Thomas – a proxy sitter who himself knew nothing about the boy. In the course of 11 sittings, the medium, Mrs Leonard, gave a total of 141 statements, which were, as I said, written down by a stenographer. When the statements were shown to Bobbie's parents, they rated the quality of the statements as follows:

Right	Good	Fair	Doubtful	Poor	Wrong
90	10	21	8	5	7

I think we can safely conclude that the method of proxy sittings, as thoroughly researched for over a century, provides, on the one hand, absolutely extraordinary evidence about what gifted mediums can do. On the other, it is a further nail in the coffin of the sceptics' attempts to explain away the phenomenon. Considering fraud for every one of the thousands of proxy sittings we have in the literature is preposterous; the very methodology of proxy sittings eliminates the possibility for the medium to employ "fishing" or "cold reading". And, by looking at the quality and quantity of the information provided, even the third and last "explanation" regularly put forward by the sceptics looks untenable.

Once it has been shown that neither fraud nor cold reading can account for the facts – what the mediums actually *do*, the last line of defence for the sceptics is to claim that mediums make such general statements that they would apply to practically anybody. An examination of the example I just cited blows this hypothesis right out of the water. There is nothing generic in Mrs Leonard's statements about Bobbie, and the same is true for any reading by truly gifted mediums.

However, as we are trying to build a rational belief in life after life, we want to be thoroughly convinced. Great examples and the impression they make on us are not enough. We want to turn, once again, to science, which is the best method we have to learn about things. And once again, I apologise if things will get a little technical. Make an effort and stay with me, please, as we briefly describe an exciting scientific adventure which has lasted now for almost 40 years.

Mediums in the laboratory

Confronted with such a preposterous claim as communicating with disincarnate personalities – "spirits" in the common parlance, our rational mind comes up with at least three key questions.

First, are the statements by the mediums precise, focussed and specific enough to actually mean something for the "sitter" (the person who consults the medium to contact a deceased loved one)? This, as I just said, is the criticism typically levelled by sceptics, who claim that statements by the mediums are intentionally vague, so that anybody – especially a bereaved person – can read something into them.

Secondly, if the statements are indeed specific and meaningful, can mediums deliver them without any previous knowledge about the disincarnates or sitters, in absence of any sensory feedback, and without using fraud or deception? As we have also seen, these are the "weapons" used by the sceptics to try to discredit what we technically define as Anomalous Information Reception (AIR).

Finally, if AIR actually takes place (which in itself I find most extraordinary and fascinating), does this information actually come from disincarnate personalities? Observers of this phenomenon have proposed that such information may be "read" by the medium from the mind of the sitter, or from some sort of "memory" embedded in the fabric of space-time.

To answer these key questions, psychical researchers have employed the most sophisticated investigation techniques already from the end of the 19th century. Through exquisitely refined research protocols and with the most rigorous controls, "historical" researchers have undoubtedly answered "yes" to all the three questions. However, this was "field" research – observing and trying to understand a phenomenon as it happens in its natural environment. It was not until some 40 years ago that mediumship research has been brought into the laboratory, an environment in which investigators have control on most – if not all – the variables of the process, and can perform quantitative, statistical analysis on the results, as it happens in any other branch of science.

We will now briefly discuss several experiments carried out by different groups on both sides of the Atlantic, looking at how protocols became increasingly sophisticated and tight in order to eliminate any possible weakness. And, we shall see how the increasingly stringent controls did not affect the results. The answer to the three questions is still a resounding "yes". As far as I am concerned, Anomalous Information Reception is proven. Period.

We begin with the investigations of Prof Archie Roy of Glasgow University and fellow physicist Tricia Robertson. First, a test was made of the sceptical hypothesis that the statements made by mediums to recipients are so general that they could as readily be accepted by non-recipients. A two-year study involving 10 mediums, 44 recipients and 407 non-recipients clearly falsified that hypothesis.

Although the original paper discusses a number of methodological intricacies to eliminate fraud and errors, the basics are simple. A medium has a public sitting with a number of people, called recipients. The statements made by the medium to individual recipients are written down. The statements are shown to the recipients who either accept them or refuse them. The same statements are subsequently shown to a control group of people, who were not present at the sitting and are called non-recipients. The members of the control group either accept them or refuse them. No matter where the experiments were carried out, no matter the manner of their recording, no matter whether the information given by the medium was at a public meeting or smaller groups throughout the UK, *the results were consistent in that there was a large gap between the number of statements accepted by recipients and by the non-recipients.*

Secondly, the researchers published the details of a strict protocol which would eliminate the possibility for the medium to get indications from body language and verbal responses from the experiments. Thirdly, the authors go on to apply the new strict protocol to a carefully designed set of experiments. The set of experiments is also designed to isolate factors, such as "Will a person accept more statements if they think or know that they are actually the recipient?" "Will a person accept fewer statements as relevant in their life if they think or know that they are not the intended recipient?" All statements are singular and the response tick is either yes or no.

This third paper covers 13 different experimental sessions carried out throughout the UK, with participants always gathered by a third party. The average number of participants at a session was approximately 25. Usually, six experiments were carried out at each session. Using statistical analysis the authors were able to evaluate the responses of every category and examine the effects, if any, of participants' beliefs on whether they were recipients or not. Even in triple (arguably quadruple) blind conditions, the intended recipients' acceptance levels continued to be higher than non-recipients, the odds against chance being *a million to one*. Very interestingly, the results incorporate all of the mediums who were used; if the authors had only given the results from the "superstars", the odds against chance would have been even greater.

No discussion of laboratory-based mediumship research would be worth much without mentioning the work Prof Gary Schwartz, Department of Psychology, University of Arizona. Over the years, Prof Schwartz and his collaborators (particularly July Beischel, who later moved on to co-found the Windbridge Institute) have consistently produced highly significant results indicating that "Anomalous Information Reception" indeed takes place, using increasingly sophisticated experimental protocols which effectively rule out the possibility of fraud, deception, sensory leakages and even telepathy as possible explanations.

It is important to stress that, similar to the studies by Roy and Roberston in Glasgow, whilst employing the most stringent protocols to eliminate conventional explanations, these experiments were also designed to maximise the potential for positive results. In particular, a) research mediums were selected after having demonstrated that they were able to perform accurately under normal mediumship or single blind conditions; b) sitters were selected to be highly motivated to receive information purportedly from their deceased loved ones and thus score the readings accurately; c) scoring systems did foster detailed item-by-item analysis of the readings, followed by meaningful summary scoring; d) experimental conditions did optimize the mediums' potential to receive information. In the words of July Beischel: "If you want to see whether a seed produces a plant, you recreate the natural conditions in which this process occurs – you do not put the seed in cement in sub-freezing temperatures".

Schwartz and Beischel published a number of papers in peer-reviewed scientific journals, both documenting their incredibly complex "blinding" procedure and reporting on the results of three replications of their laboratory experiments. "Blinding" refers to the fact that, as Beischel famously said, "Nobody knows anything about anything". In the case of the proxy sittings we described earlier there are at least two levels of blinding: the medium knows nothing about the spirit he or she is expected to communicate with, and the proxy sitter knows nothing about the spirit either. If the sitter doesn't even know the person, related to the spirit, who initially requested the sitting, there are three levels of blinding. Complicated stuff, eh?

Now, imagine that the last paper by the two researchers, published in 2007, reported on a *quintuple blind* experimental protocol: there are *five levels of separation* between the medium and the spirit he or she is expected to communicate with. The experiments involved eight sitters who had experienced a recent bereavement and eight mediums who had previously demonstrated to be able to perform in normal conditions as well as under single- and double-blind conditions. All eight mediums carried out readings for all eight spirits. At the end of the experiment, when all readings were done and the mediums' statements collected, each sitter received not one, but two lists of statements: one was the "correct" one, referring to the spirit he or she wanted to hear from, and the other was "incorrect", a decoy from the reading for another spirit, used for control purposes. Obviously, sitters didn't know which list of statements was which (that is one of the five levels of blinding).

Each sitter then scored the reading intended for him/her as well as the control according to a six-point scale ranging from 6 (Excellent reading, including strong aspects of communication, and with essentially no incorrect information) to 0 (No correct information or communication). On the whole, the average summary rating was significantly higher for the intended readings than for the controls. It is noteworthy that three mediums produced dramatic findings, with summary scores of 5.0 and 5.5 across the eight readings; two mediums produced moderate findings (summary scores of 3.5); and none of the mediums produced reversals (i.e., control ratings higher than intended ratings).

Finally, sitters were asked to pick the reading which seems to be more applicable to him or her. Here too, results were very positive, with sitters picking the right statement 81% of the cases.

In summary, this study confirms and extends the results obtained previously with less sophisticated (single- and double-blind) protocols: there appears to be some sort of anomalous information reception mechanism operating during mediumship readings. Research mediums are indeed capable of providing *accurate* and *specific* information about a deceased person *when all possible communication channels with the sitter are closed.*

…and if you have skipped some parts above because they are too technical, please read this next section

To conclude this brief review of lab experiments, let me tell you about another interesting study carried out by Emily Williams Kelly and Dianne Arcangel, and published in 2011 by the prestigious *Journal of Nervous and Mental Diseases*.

The substance of the study is pretty much the same as in the experiments we have described earlier. 9 mediums and 40 sitters took part in this exercise. The two authors acted as proxy sitters, so that the mediums were blind as to who the intended recipient was. The mediums were given just a photograph of the deceased person, and nothing else – no name, no age of death. The mediums' readings were taped and then transcribed, removing any references to the appearance of the person in the photograph or any other such clues. Each sitter was then sent 6 transcripts – the real one, as well as 5 intended for other persons, all 6 selected from the same age and gender group. The sitters ranked the transcripts from 1 to 6, 1 being the most accurate.

As in previous studies, the results were highly significant: 14 of the 38 readings were correctly chosen, and 7 others were ranked second. Altogether, 30 of the 38 were ranked in the top half. Statistically, the probability of obtaining such results by chance is less than one in 10,000. This study indicates again that mediums are indeed capable of providing information about a deceased person whilst all known channels of communication are closed, and that the results were not due to chance or over interpretation of generic statements.

However, what is really interesting in this particular study is that the authors have looked not only at the quantitative aspects, but also at the qualitative ones. These are equally important, not only because of the emotional impact they often have on the bereaved person, but also because they may give us more insight into the kind of information more likely to come through.

Most of the 14 people who correctly chose their own reading made comments such as "I don't see how it could be anything other than (X reading)"; "I feel certain this is the correct choice and would bet my life on it"; "one reading stood out from the rest . . .. I just know (it) was correct because it sounded like my mom"; "it had the most instances that could apply to my son."

In addition to such general statements, however, some did go on to comment on specific details that impressed them. For example, the person who "would bet my life" on his choice cited the medium's statement that "there's something funny about black liquorice . . .. Like there's a big joke about it, like, ooh, you like that?" According to the sitter, his deceased son and his wife had joked about liquorice frequently. Also, the medium had said "I also have sharp pain in the rear back of the left side of my head in the back, in the occipital. So perhaps there was an injury back there, or he hit something or something hit him." The deceased person had died of such an injury incurred in a car crash.

In another reading, the medium said "I feel like the hair I see here in the photo is gone, so I have to go with cancer or something that would take the hair away," and later "her hair—at some point she's kind of teasing it, she tried many colours. I think she experimented with colour a lot before her passing." The girl's mother confirmed that she had died of cancer, had dyed her hair "hot pink" before her surgery, and had later shaved her head when her hair began falling out (her hair was normal-looking in the photo.).

In another example, among many other details the sitter commented especially on the statement "He said 'I don't know why they keep that clock if they are not going to make it work.' So somebody connected directly to him has a clock that either is not wound up, or they let it run down, or it's standing there just quiet. And he said 'What's the point in having a clock that isn't running?' So, somebody should know about that and it should give them quite a laugh." The sitter did laugh (and cry) over this, because a grandfather clock that her husband had kept wound had not been wound since his death. The medium had also commented that "he can be on a soap box, hammering it". His children when young had frequently complained about "Dad being on his soap box".

The article cites many other such examples. These kinds of anecdotes are nothing new to anybody who has studied mediumship or had a sitting with a good medium. I very much welcome the fact that these particular ones were published in a top peer-reviewed scientific publication, along with convincing statistical results.

A good reading by a medium substantially reduces grief in the bereaved

The last piece of research I would like to bring to your attention is one of the several studies carried out on the effect of various forms of after-death communication on the grief experienced by those who have lost a loved one. This piece of research was carried out by Julie Beischel, PhD, and Marc Boccuzzi, of the Windbridge Institute in the US. These researchers asked a group of 83 recently and less-recently bereaved persons to self-evaluate their levels of grief before and a after sitting with one of the Institute's research mediums using a specially designed questionnaire. Not unsurprisingly – as this finding is consistent with those of all the other studies carried out on the subject – participants reported a marked and statistically significant reduction in their levels of grief. What was particularly interesting in this particular study was that the researchers did not stop at the quantitative measurements of the effects. They added a simple, open-ended question at the end of the questionnaire: "Do you have any other comments about your grief that you would like to share with the investigators?" The answers are strongly indicative – even more so than the statistical results – of the potential therapeutic benefit of after-death communication.

The following representative comments were provided regarding the short-and long-term effects of a mediumship reading on the experience of grief:

> "After the reading I felt tremendously upbeat. This euphoria lasted the whole day. It was very amazing."

> "Before my reading with [the medium], I still had a low level of grief . . . that I accepted as the loss that will always be there. After the reading, I felt as though that "weight" was lifted and I had a different definition of my relationship with my mom that was more special than I could ever expect."

> "When I am approached by my loved one that has passed, I am much more accepting of her presence and look forward to the joy instead of the pain... I wish I had had the reading 16 years ago!"

> "[The medium] and her gift of mediumship has had a profound effect on my life and my grieving process. ... It has helped me in a way I never would have imagined."

"It is very healing for me to use mediums for help in this process .I believe going to a good medium is an untapped resource for faster grief management."

"[The medium] helped me manage the grief that has been with me for more than 20 years"

"I feel a reading with a medium is an excellent tool for helping to decrease grief... I would recommend it to anyone that is considering it."

"I don't know what I would have done without [the medium]"

In conclusion, I hope that this third, long and somewhat technical "substantive" chapter of this book helped you realise that after-death communication is a real thing and that, most importantly, that the communicators who speak to us from the spirit world through mediums and other channels are indeed who they claim to be. They once lived on earth, in the material world, and now live in a nonmaterial dimension which awaits us all, and retain all the characteristics that made them "themselves" during earthly life.

Chapter seven
Before we die

After long investigations into various features of and issues surrounding our three main sources of information, it is finally the time to reach the aim of this whole book: to provide you, the reader, with a description of what happens towards the end of life, at the moment of death, and afterwards. In attempting to do so, I am all too conscious of the fact that "death mapping" is far from an exact science. Unfortunately, we cannot send our scientists with the measuring devices into these otherworldly realms – not even a documentarist, or a guy with a mobile phone to take a few pictures! Therefore, as I have been saying from the beginning, we have to rely on the testimony of people who have made the transition, and for this reason we have spent so much time in an effort to establish their credibility.

Rather than attempting a description myself based on the testimony from our sources, therefore, I decided to let them speak for themselves. My job has been to select a good number of quotes, and to provide a minimum of context for each, when applicable. The selection job has not been easy, as, here too, the sheer mass of testimony is enormous. Especially, though, I had to make an effort in selecting the quotes (or "reports", if you want), so that most resemble each other in terms of language and themes. This is a crucial subject, and it is essential that you understand it well.

If you look at the testimony on the afterlife as a whole, you are bound to find a considerable deal of diversity. People belonging different cultures, living in different parts of the world and at different times during the last two centuries inevitably describe things differently. Moreover, and even more importantly, different people are bound to describe essentially the same experience in different ways. This becomes immediately understandable if you consider ten people who go on holiday to Paris, in France, and are asked to provide a short report upon their return. They have all been to the same place, but would you expect them to report exactly the same things? Of course not. There would obviously be a number of common themes (everybody would talk about the Tour Eiffel and the Louvre museum, for instance) but a lot of details would differ depending on the individual experience each of the travellers had.

This is exactly what happens with the process of dying and the afterlife. There certainly are common themes (so much so that we are comfortable in drawing generalisations and come up with a "map", or general structure, of the nonmaterial universe, with its different levels and corresponding experiences) but a lot of the more personal details in the descriptions vary. It is my hope that my work of selection and my attempted "systematisation" in presenting the testimony will help you forming a reasonably clear picture.

It will therefore be *your* job to read (and, I suggest, re-read) with attention the many case stories and the quotes and the testimony I assembled in the following chapters, to reflect and meditate on them, and to put together a general description of the dying process and the afterlife which, I hope and believe, you will find extraordinarily comforting.

Finally, before we begin, by looking at what happens in the hours before the moment of transition, let me say a word about the sources I will be using (I mean sources in bibliographic terms). This not being an academic text, and since the remaining chapters are literally packed with quotes, I have decided not to provide a bibliographic reference for each of them. I thought few of my intended readers would really be interested in that, and doing so would render the text a lot less reader-friendly. However, in the Appendix, I have listed all the books and publications I have consulted during my selection process. Any reader interested in going into further depth will find enormous quantities of material there.

From this chapter onwards, before digging into the testimony from our trusted sources concerning each step of the end-of-life to afterlife transition, I will try to capture the very essence of what the testimony tells us with a simple statement. In the case of deathbed vision, I would like to say that

Contrary to what most people fear, we do not die alone.

Please reflect and meditate on this very important statement. As you will go through the testimony and the case studies in the next pages, you will realise to what extent this statement is true. This realisation, in itself, can go some length in transforming your fear of death.

The first story about the period immediately preceding death comes from Sir William Barrett, a professor of physics at the Royal College of Science in Dublin in the 1920s. The story, actually, is about something his wife witnessed – events that made a great impression on him, to the point that he went on to become one of the most prominent psychical researchers of his time.

Sir William's wife was a gynaecologist at Dublin's main hospital and, on the night of January 12, 1924, she arrived home from the hospital eager to tell her husband about a case she had had that day. She had been called into the operating room to deliver the child of a woman named Doris (her last name was withheld from the written report). Although the child was born healthy, Doris was dying from a haemorrhage. As the doctors waited helplessly next to the dying woman, she began to see things. As Lady Barrett tells it:

> "Suddenly she looked eagerly towards part of the room, a radiant smile illuminating her whole countenance. 'Oh, lovely, lovely,' she said. I asked, 'What is lovely?' 'What I see,' she replied in low, intense tones. 'What do you see?' 'Lovely brightness, wonderful beings.'
>
> It is difficult to describe the sense of reality conveyed by her intense absorption in the vision. Then - seeming to focus her attention more intently on one place for a moment - she exclaimed, almost with a kind of joyous

cry, 'Why, it's Father! Oh, he's so glad I'm coming; he is so glad. It would be perfect if only W. (her husband) would come too.'

Her baby was brought for her to see. She looked at it with interest, and then said, 'Do you think I ought to stay for baby's sake?' Then, turning toward the vision again, she said, 'I can't - I can't stay; if you could see what I do, you would know I can't stay.'

Now – Sir William was a scientist, and as such the first objection he made to his wife concerning this apparently compelling story was that it was nothing more than a hallucination due to lack of blood or triggered by fear of death. Then he heard the rest of the story. It seems that the sister of Doris, Vida, had died only three weeks earlier. Since Doris was in such delicate condition, the death of her beloved sister was kept a secret from her. That is why the final part of her deathbed vision was so amazing to Barrett.

"She spoke to her father, saying: 'I am coming,' turning at the same time to look at me, saying, 'Oh, he is so near.' On looking at the same place again, she said with a rather puzzled expression: 'He has Vida with him,' turning again to me saying, 'Vida is with him.' Then she said, 'You do want me, Dad; I am coming.'"

This is indeed one of the many, well documented cases in which a deathbed vision (DBV) includes somebody the dying person *didn't know was dead at the moment the vision took place.*

In a similar way, Prof Barrett further reported on a case involving a young girl who was dying of consumption and had been seemingly unconscious and unaware of things going on around her when she opened her eyes and uttered the names of her three sisters, who had all died, as if recognizing their presence. Then, after a short pause, she said, "and Edward, too." At the time, Edward, her brother, was thought to be alive in India, but word was later received that he had died in an accident a week or so prior to his sister's vision. "The evidence seems indisputable that, in some cases, just before death the veil is partly drawn aside and glimpses of the loved ones who have passed over is given to the dying person." Barrett concluded.

Our second story comes from Reverend Arthur Chambers, vicar of the Church of England in Brockenhurst, Hampshire, England, who reported that a dying man said to him, "You consider, do you not, that my mind is perfectly clear?" Chambers assured him that he did and that he had never known him to be more so. "Very well, then," the dying man continued. "Now I want to tell you what occurred last evening. But first you must understand that I was neither dreaming nor under a delusion. As I lay here, my father, who died some years ago, stood in the place where you are now and spoke to me. He told me I had only a very little longer to remain on earth, and said that he and other dear ones passed away were waiting to welcome me into the spiritual world. I tried to raise myself in bed, in order to attract the attention of the nurse who was at the other end of the ward. I thought you might still be in the building, and I wanted her to send for you, that you, too, might see my father. I supposed the effort to raise myself must have been too much for me, for I slipped back on the pillow and felt I was fainting. When I opened my eyes again, I looked for my father, but he was gone. Don't tell me I was dreaming, because I tell you with my dying breath I was not. My father was as real there as you are now, and I think he will come again." The man died two days later, after which Chambers spoke to a man in a nearby bed. Without knowing what the dying man had told Chambers, the patient informed Chambers that just before the man died he saw him raise himself into a sitting position, fix his gaze earnestly on the spot where Chambers had so often prayed and conversed with him, smile, as if he were recognizing someone, and then fall back on his pillow motionless.

Dr Reginald Hegy, an Irish physician reported a deathbed scene which left a lasting impression on him. It involved an elderly woman, who had been comatose and was expected to die at any time.

> Most unexpectedly a period of consciousness ensued when those around the bedside were surprised to hear the patient calmly state that she had just seen her

husband who had died thirty years previously, and had been told that her time to pass over had not yet come and that she would remain on earth three days longer," Hegy recorded. "She also gave a message to her nurse (a widow), which she said was from this lady's deceased husband. The message proved to be remarkably relevant. After this period of lucidity the state of unconsciousness again supervened, and lasted three days, at the end of which time death took place as the patient had herself foretold.

In her book *They Walked Among Us,* Louie Harris recalled the passing of her father. He whispered to his wife that it was time for him to leave and apologized for not being able to bid farewell to Ted, their son, who was serving in the British army in France. "Father was quiet for some time," Harris wrote. "His eyes were closed. Then, quite unexpectedly, he sat up unaided, his eyes open, his face radiant. He stretched out his arms and joyfully exclaimed: 'George! Austin!' These were the names of his 'dead' brothers. A beautiful smile transformed his thin face. With a deep sigh of satisfaction he lay back on his pillow and passed peacefully to the spirit world."

Likewise, in a moving 2015 TED talk, Christopher Kerr, the chief medical officer at the Center for Hospice and Palliative Care in Buffalo, showed a clip of one his terminally ill patients discussing her deathbed visions, which included her saying, "My mom and dad, my uncle, everybody I knew that was dead was there [by my side]. I remember seeing every piece of their face." She was lucid and present.

Anita, a social worker at a major hospital in the US, tells the story of one of Felicia, one of the patients she assisted:

> At some stage, Felicia stopped talking completely, not because her hearing was diminishing or that she just didn't want to, but because even the simple act of speaking exhausted her beyond belief. When it was clear to everyone that she was very close to dying, her family

gathered and took turns watching over her. I was there to provide them with whatever assistance I could. She continued her silence until one day she suddenly sat up, very primlike, and waved at her daughter to look towards where she was pointing.

"Don't you see them?" Felicia asked. Her voice sounded clear as a bell, and her breathing was steady and even for the first time in many months.

"See who?"

"I see a dock; and there are your dad, grandmother, grandfather, and uncle."

"I still don't see them." Carole, the daughter, said.

"Well, they're all there!" he mother exclaimed. "They're standing on the dock, waiting for me to come across." She paused, and then spoke directly to those she was gazing upon: "There's no boat at the dock. How can I get to you?"

Carole had no clue how to answer her. I didn't know what to say myself, but I did know Felicia's question was not for us and that she'd find the answer when the time came.

The following day, Felicia quietly uttered, "The boat is finally at the pier." Those were her last words. In the end, she died peacefully.

A similar account comes from Heather, an American nurse, whose elderly father and mother lived in two different nursing homes. As it was clear that the mother was nearing the end:

> I was searching for a way for my parents to be together, but my mother's facility didn't accept Alzheimer's patients, while my father's *only* accepted patients with Alzheimer's and dementia. We weren't sure if we

should even tell him how bad Mom was doing because there basically was nothing he could do. We'd hoped to find a way to get him out for a few hours to see his wife when the call came that Mom's conditions had worsened: her blood pressure was dropping and her heart rate was increasing.

That evening, my family and I sat by my Mom, who was still very alert, but her breathing was more audible than usual. She suddenly looked up and said, "Joseph died. Why didn't anybody tell me this?"

I jumped in and quickly corrected her, "Mom, Daddy isn't dead, He is still in the nursing home."

Startled by her statement, I realised that I'd better find a way to get Dad over here. We were afraid that my Mom was beginning to lose her faculties, and we wanted her to see her husband while she still could talk to him.

"Mom," I said, "we'll see if the nursing home will let us pick up Dad so he can visit." I nodded to my cousin Jackie to call the nursing home and make arrangements for one of us to get him.

"Joseph already came to say good-bye," Mom insisted, "and he told me that I'd be with him soon."

We all just looked at each other, acknowledging that my mother was hallucinating. I gently repeated, "Mom, Dad is in the nursing home, we're going to bring him here."

Once again she repeated, "No, he's dead," but this time she also sat up. "Look, there he is!" She seemed to be gazing past everybody, and then she said, "Joseph, you came back for me." Her eyes filled with tears and she lay back on the bed.

Just then a nurse and my cousin motioned for me to come over and talk to them at the nurses' station. I met them just outside the door when Jackie said, "Heather, I don't know how to tell you this. I called the nursing home, and Joseph died about 15 minutes ago. He had a heart attack."

Mom died two days later. Even though I hadn't seen the vision of my father, I found great comfort in the fact that he had come to my mother, and now they were together again.

Another one of these intriguing accounts comes from Natalie Kalmus, known for her work on colour cinematography, who reported that her dying sister, who was not under the influence of any drugs, lifted herself almost into a sitting position and spoke of the presence of many unseen visitors. "There are so many of them… Fred… and Ruth… what's she doing here? Oh, I know… So many of them … I'm going up." Again, the reference to Ruth was particularly moving for Natalie Kalmus, as Ruth was a cousin who had died suddenly the week before, and whose death was unknown to the dying woman.

It is also fascinating to note that DBVs do not only include visions of departed relatives. Quite a number of them hint at the vision of wondrous otherworldly realms, and this, as we will see in one of the next chapters, resonates perfectly with what NDErs and spirit communicators tell us about one of the "levels" of the spirit world. Apple's founder Steve Job's very famous last words, on his deathbed moments before passing, were "Wow! Wow! Wow!".

Quite a few years before that, Roberta Hutchinson, the Assistant Matron at the Saskatchewan Indian Hospital in Canada, wrote about a patient she saw at the moment of his death:

> At last the supreme day arrived. It was evening and I was with him. He was lying quietly in his bed when suddenly he sat up, stretched forth his arms with a yearning gesture, while an ecstatic smile broke over his face. It was not simply a smile of pleasure, but something far beyond it. The veil was lifted, and no one who was looking on could fail to realize that it was a

glorious vision that met his gaze. He then lay back in his bed, looked at me with a smile, and passed away. He had been calm and collected during the day, there was no delirium; it was an unclouded glimpse of that higher life into which he was just entering.

Dr Paul Edwards, a medical doctor in California describes the following episode saying, "I think of all my death scenes, this was the most impressive, the most solemn."

I was called upon to visit a very dear lady friend who was very low and weak from consumption. Everyone knew that this pure and noble wife and mother was doomed to die, and at last she herself became convinced that immediate death was inevitable, and accordingly she prepared for the event. Calling her children to her bedside she kissed each in turn, sending them away as soon as good-bye was said. Then came the husband's turn to step up and bid farewell to a most loving wife, who was perfectly clear in her mind. She began by saying, "Newton," (for that was his Christian name) "do not weep over me, for I am without pain and am wholly serene. I love you upon earth, and shall love you after I have gone. I am fully resolved to come to you if such a thing is possible, and if it is not possible I will watch you and the children from Heaven, where I will be waiting when you all come. My first desire now is to go... I see people moving - all in white. The music is strangely enchanting. Oh! Here is Sadie; she is with me - and - she knows who I am." Sadie was a little girl she had lost about ten years before. "Sissy!" said the husband, "you are out of your mind." "Oh, dear! Why did you call me here again?" said the wife, "now it will be hard for me to go away again; I was so pleased while there. It was so delightful - so soothing." In about three minutes the dying woman added, "I am going away again and will not come back to you even if you call me."

This scene lasted for about eight minutes, and it was very plain that the dying wife was in full view of the two worlds at the same time, for she described how the moving figures looked in the world beyond, as she directed her words to mortals in this world.

In concluding this brief review of deathbed visions, I would like to add a few considerations of my own.

First, the number of case reports I selected is relatively small. To be sure, I could have gone on and on, for there is an incredible abundance of published material about this subject. The reason why I didn't do so is that the accounts of the visions are very, very similar to each other. No matter where in the world they come from, and in what period of the last couple of centuries they were collected, they all follow the same pattern. I therefore thought there was not much to be gained by going through a longer series of essentially identical accounts.

Secondly, I have intentionally chosen several cases in which the dying person reports seeing somebody he or she didn't know was dead at the moment the vision takes place. These cases are not very frequent, and certainly a lot less frequent than one could imagine by looking at my selection. Yet, they are there, and they have been very thoroughly investigated. The reason why I selected a relatively higher percentage of those is that they appear to close the door on any discussion on the nature of DBVs. The *only* possible explanation for these cases is that the dying person actually enters into contact with a discarnate personality inhabiting a different dimension of existence. And, by implication, discarnate personalities *do exist*, which means that *human personality survives bodily death.*

Thirdly, I was hoping to find more accounts in which the dying person describes visions of the afterlife. These accounts are there, but they are not numerous and the descriptions tend to be limited to a few words. Very interestingly, even those few words describe a wondrous environment, essentially anybody's idea of what Heaven could be, and this is *exactly* what NDErs do in their accounts, and *exactly* how spirit communicators describe one of the levels in which the spirit world appears to be divided. Once more – as I discussed in the introductory chapter on evidence – it is the coherence and consistency among accounts coming from very different sources that enormously adds credibility to what we hear.

Finally, people having DBVs do not talk much about the environment they sometimes peek into primarily because they are interested in *people*. I find this the most profound, moving aspect of deathbed visions. Most people – I daresay practically everybody – are scared of dying alone. I am writing this chapter as the second wave of the COVID-19 pandemic is ravaging many countries of Europe, and I know that death by this particular infection is particularly horrible. People actually do die alone, generally after a long period of intense, harrowing discomfort, also spent alone, without the comfort of family and friends. I find the thought of these deaths, on the one hand, very difficult to bear. On the other, I take comfort from knowing that, as I said in the beginning and as indicated by thousands upon thousands of accounts of deathbed visions, *we actually die surrounded by our loved ones.* We are not alone. And, at that stage, we are actually happy and willing to take the last step into a new reality that looks warm, bright, marvellous and intensely welcoming.

Chapter eight
The moment of death

As I did I the previous chapter, I would like to try to encapsulate what we learn from our sources concerning the moment of death with a short statement, on which you should ideally reflect and meditate before digging into the testimony and case studies. In this case, the statement is slightly longer, as it contains not one but two fundamental truths, both essential for the transformation of our fear of death.

Contrary to what most people fear, the death of the body is not the end of life.

Whilst the process leading up to it can involve much suffering, the moment of death is subjectively perceived as unnoticeable at worst and as liberation and a joy at best.

Now, I believe that, instinctively, most of us think of death as a black curtain that falls and puts an end to everything – our being alive, our being conscious, our having feelings and memories. Basically like falling into a dreamless sleep, or slipping into the drugs-induced coma of anaesthesia before surgery. Only, having died, we won't wake up – that's the end of it, just blackness and nothingness. This is, I believe, the most fundamental of human fears – the fear of annihilation, of ceasing to exist. Perhaps, this is precisely the kind of fear that has brought you to this book.

I trust that, having read what I have been writing up to this point, you already have a pretty good idea that annihilation and ceasing to exist is definitely *not* what appears to be happening when our bodies cease functioning. However, I also believe that you, like anybody else, is curious and somewhat apprehensive about the very moment of death. Is it painful? Distressing? Unpleasant? What happens to us when we cross the threshold? Well, the somewhat underwhelming answer is... *nothing!* The moment of transition appears absolutely featureless. If anything is felt at all, it is a welcome end of the physical suffering some of us go through in the terminal part of our lives. One spirit communicator reflects exactly on this:

> "They do not suffer, these people, in their passing. I think sometimes their friends suffer more, when they see the bodies writhing in apparent agony, while in reality the spirit is already tasting the first freedom from pain, or lies in a blessed insensibility."

True to the format of this crucial section of the book, I will now continue to let those who actually *have made* that transition describe what goes on.

Let's begin with renowned psychologist Karl Novotny, who had died in Germany in 1965. He came through his long-time friend Grete Schroeder, who had suddenly and unexpectedly shown automatic writing capabilities, producing lessons of psychology and psychiatry, subjects totally unknown to the medium, an accountant by profession. Asked by Schroeder to describe the process of dying, Novotny said:

> "It was a spring day, and I was in my country residence, where I rarely go. My health was poor, but I didn't feel the need to stay in bed - on the contrary, I decided to go on a walk with some friends. It was a beautiful evening. Suddenly, I felt very tired and I thought I could not go on. I made an effort to continue, and, all of a sudden, I felt healthy and rested. I quickened my pace, and took in the evening fresh air: I hadn't felt that good in a long time. What happened? Suddenly, I could feel neither tiredness nor the usual laboured breath. I went back towards the friends, who had stopped, and what did I see? I saw myself lying on the ground! My friends were

agitated and desperate; one ran to find a doctor. I got near my "other self" lying on the ground and I looked for the heartbeat: there was no doubt – I was dead! But I felt more alive than ever! I tried to talk to my friends, but they didn't even look at me or bother answering.

So I got angry and went away, but an instant later I was back. It wasn't a pretty sight: all my friends, in tears, who were not taking any notice of me; and that dead body, identical to me, although I felt very good. My dog was yapping in agitation and could not decide whether to come to me or to the other one lying on the ground… When all formalities were dealt with and my body was put in a coffin I understood I was really dead. I couldn't believe it! I went to see my colleagues at the University, but they could not see me either and didn't answer to my calls. What should I do? I went up the hill where Grete lives. I saw her, alone and sad, but she couldn't see me either. I had to surrender to the truth. The very moment I realized I had left the material world, I saw my mother coming to me with an overjoyed expression on her face and telling me I was in the afterlife."

Accounts from Near-Death Experiencers (NDErs) gathered in detail during the last 60 years describe with near-identical words the moment in which the "spirit", "soul" or "etheric body" (as it is variously been referred to by different sources) separates from the dying body. Typically, NDErs tend to find themselves in the room above the body, often in a corner, looking down at their prostrate form as if they were a spectator. They usually state that at the time this seemed quite natural, and also report a heightened but detached mental process, more acute hearing, and a very brightly illuminated environment. This situation is described as being distinctly real. They feel as much alive as before, in fact many of the respondents reported feeling more alive and were conscious of everything that was happening. Let's remind ourselves that during this period the individual can be observed to have reached the stage of brain death, with complete cessation of neurological function, deep unconsciousness without response to painful stimuli and without any EEG electrical activity. The following accounts are typical of this phase of the experience. A woman recalled her heart attack as follows:

> "I was in the intensive care unit of Worthing hospital. During the early hours, I found myself suspended above my body looking down at myself. I heard and saw two doctors and a nurse running towards the bed and heard them say 'quick, quick'. I am sure I had died."

And a woman who had nearly died as a result of complications which developed after a tonsillectomy observed:

> "I remember that absolutely beautiful feeling of peace and happiness. I was above, I don't know where, but I was definitely up. I didn't have a body, but at the same time it was definitely up there."

A woman who was suffering from hyperventilation recalled:

> "I was with a neighbour arranging to have my children looked after as I was feeling so unwell and I wanted my husband to take me to my doctor. Suddenly for no reason I got a severe pain and muscle spasm down the left side of my body, with a burning sensation. I called out to my friend and as she came into the room I collapsed onto the floor. Then everything went black. I opened my eyes but everything was still black. I could hear quite clearly and knew I was not unconscious. Then suddenly I realised I was standing up by the door and could see my body lying on the floor. I could see everything that was going on. I was convinced that I was dying as my heart felt as if it had stopped beating, whereas before it had been pounding. Also the pain had ceased."

The cessation of pain and suffering seems a common theme when describing the transition between life and afterlife. The spirit of Abraham Ackley, a medical doctor from Cleveland Ohio, communicating through a medium reported that:

"I experienced but very little suffering during the last instants of my life, though at first there were struggles and my features were distorted; but I learned, after my spirit had burst its barriers and was freed from its connection with the external body, that these were produced by it in an attempt to sever this connection, which in all cases is more or less difficult; the vital points of contact being suddenly broken by disease, the union in other parts of the system is necessarily severed with violence, but, as far as I have experienced, without consciousness of pain. Like many others, I found that I was unable to leave the form at once. I could feel myself gradually raised from my body, and in a dreamy, half-conscious state. My spirit was freed a short time after the organs of my physical body had entirely ceased to perform their functions. My spiritual form was then united into one, and I was raised a short distance above the body, standing over it by what power I was unable to tell. I could see those who were in the room around me, and knew by what was going on that considerable time must have elapsed since dissolution had taken place. I presume I must have been for a time unconscious; and this I find is a common experience, not however, universal."

Communicating through South African trance medium Nina Merrington, Mike Swain, who died in an auto accident, told his father Jesper Swain, a noted South African lawyer, that he left his body an instant before the cars actually impacted. Heather, his fiancée's young sister, was also killed in the accident. Mike told of being blinded by the glare of the sun reflecting on the windscreen of the oncoming car, and then:

"All of a sudden, the radiance changes from silver to gold. I am being lifted up in the air, out through the top of the car. I grab little Heather's hand. She too is being lifted out of the car. When we are about 30 feet above the car, we witness the collision below us. There is a noise like the snapping of steel banjo strings. We feel no pain whatsoever."

Sir Alvary Gascoigne, a diplomat, addressing his wife through a medium enthusiastically declared:

> "Every part of me seemed to be switching off gently, and... I suddenly found I was floating above my body ... Nothing in life comes close to the immense joy of dying ... I told you that I had experienced a strange feeling of power that seemed to be drawing me out of my body during the last few days of my illness ... I welcomed this inrush of new life and let go very willingly ... you must be ready to receive the power that draws you quite painlessly out of your body. It's the most beautiful and glorious thing."

Back to testimony from NDErs we can briefly explore how different persons experience their nonmaterial "body". A woman who was haemorrhaging following an operation for the removal of fibroids in her womb related:

> "I remember coming round from the anaesthetic and then drifting off and finding myself out of my body, over the bed looking down at my carcass. I was aware only of being a brain and eyes, I do not remember having a body. The next thing I realised was that I was neither a woman nor a man, just pure spirit. I could see the doctors and nurses round my bed frantically trying to give me a blood transfusion. They were having difficulty finding a vein in my arm. I was amused at all this fuss going on with my body as it did not concern me a bit."

Although this woman could see her body quite clearly, she was nevertheless not aware of being in another body as such, but rather, she was conscious only of being an entity. This sense of being in some sort of formless dimension is reported by many of the experiencers during this phase, but while they do not seem to have any recognisable form, they are still very much conscious of being themselves. A man who had been in hospital undergoing treatment for leukaemia also referred to this sense of spiritual identity:

> "I became aware of my spirit, or whatever you want to call it, being up in a corner of the room and looking down on my body with doctors and nurses, and all the people and hospital paraphernalia being brought into the room and piled on my chest and so forth. I could not feel any of this at the time it was happening, but I was like a spectator looking down on this from up in the corner of the room. I didn't have any regrets or anything, it just felt kind of strange."

After having left their physical body, some NDErs and spirit communicators report early encounters with deceased loved ones or other discarnate entities. For instance, the spirit of one Jim Nolan, who died in a typhoid epidemic during the American secession war, speaking through medium Mrs Hollis, explains:

> "It was like waking up from a sleep, only with a feeling of bewilderment. I didn't feel ill anymore, and that surprised my greatly. I had a feeling something weird had happened, but couldn't understand exactly what. My body was lying on the bed of the field hospital and I could see it. I told myself 'What a weird phenomenon!' I look around and saw three of my comrades who were killed in the trench and whom I had buried myself. And still, they were there, in front of me! I looked at them with astonishment and one of them greeted me saying: 'Hello Jim, welcome to the spirit world'. I was deeply shaken and said, 'My God, what are you saying? I'm not dead...!' 'No', said the other, 'you are more alive than before. But you are in the spirit world. All you have to do to convince yourself is look at your body'."

Frances Banks, a nun, is an interesting example of somebody who had a deathbed vision before she passed (her last few words were "The Change has started") *and* communicated through a medium after passing. She talks of her first impressions after death:

> "After the Change was over and I was free of my earthly 'covering' I woke up here . ... I opened my eyes, or I came back to consciousness ... and there was Mother Superior just as she used to be and as I had remembered her for so many years. She took my hand. She said 'So you have arrived safely?'"

Although in near-death experiences the encounter with discarnate personalities generally happens further along in the process, some do get very early interactions, which generally have to do with the fact that their moment for the final transition hasn't come yet and they have to go back into their physical body. A student who was nearly asphyxiated during a bout of croup remembered having this experience:

> "I was very ill and had great difficulty breathing. One evening I woke about nine o'clock from sleep realising something was prompting me to wake up and I realised I could not breathe. My eyes were popping out of my head and I was aware I was being asphyxiated. I can remember trying to rouse my sister who was asleep in the same room with me, but as I couldn't breathe this wasn't possible. I told myself to relax and accept that I was unable to breathe and just lay there waiting to die. By this time I was unable to close my eyes. Then I realised that I was starting to move upwards towards the ceiling and I thought I was going to bang myself on the ceiling at any minute and turned to avoid hitting the ceiling and as I did so I saw myself lying on the bed and I thought I looked very ill, terrible with great bags under my eyes. I felt weightless and I somehow moved through the ceiling which was no longer important. I was aware of going faster and faster. I wasn't frightened; but I wondered where I was going. Suddenly I heard a stern male voice above me which said, 'Get back, get back in there.' With that I found myself back in bed in a split second. I have no idea how I got there but I gasped for breath and sat up coughing blood. I managed to rouse my sister and told her what had happened but she

said it was obviously because I was feverish. But I know the experience was totally real."

The woman we mentioned before who was in Charing Cross Hospital after an attack of hyperventilation stated, "Next I heard a voice, which I am sure was my mother's, saying, 'No, you must go back.'" Another woman, who endured prolonged labour giving birth said, "At this point I heard a man's voice, it was not anyone I recognised, saying, 'You must go back.' It was a kind voice but very firm and he was saying, 'Remember the baby, who's going to look after it? You must go back.'" And a woman who was taken unconscious to hospital suffering from a fractured skull after being knocked down by a car reported, "Then I heard a voice, it was not an English voice, but it sounded foreign, saying, 'Margaret, go back, go back.' I next felt as if a blind was pulled down and I shot back into my conscious state and woke up in the hospital bed."

Finally, some NDErs also report, immediately after living their physical body, experiences which typically occur at a later stage – visions of great brightness, vivid colours and even glimpses of the wonderful environment we'll describe later as "wonderland". For instance, a second hyperventilation case who had been treated in the cardiac ward of Charing Cross Hospital observed: "I suddenly became aware I was floating above myself and all the fear and panic seemed to go. I was calm and everything was very bright. I felt peaceful and warm. It was really beautiful." And a woman who was in intensive care for twelve days following a serious car accident said: "During this time I was surrounded by lovely soft glowing colours."

And, in an account which is typical of the "wonderland" stage of the process, an NDEr reported:

> "To my astonishment, I saw my mum and dad standing only a few steps from me. They were smiling at me (note that I had never really known my mum as she died when I was very young) and they were not talking, but I

understood they were telling me not to be afraid. Behind them there was a vast plain, immersed in light, a light of peace, which you understand is eternal, in which living is sweet, a light no human words could even begin to describe."

Chapter nine

The early afterlife

Before we proceed to look at the testimony concerning the next step in the after-death process, I need to introduce a very important concept, one which has been dealt with by a few important spiritual traditions in the past, and one which appears constantly in the accounts we receive from spirit communicators. In fact, the concepts are two, and apparently separate; in reality, I believe they are sides of the same coin. They are strictly related, as the first is heavily influenced by the second. Here they are:

What happens in the early stages of life in the spirit world depends largely on the psychological state and beliefs of the person having made the transition.

If we want to call the part of ourselves that survives "soul", then there are "younger", "less experienced" souls and "older", more mature and experienced souls. This too has a significant impact on the early stages of the spirit life.

I understand that, for somebody who's never heard these things before, the first concept may be somewhat easier to accept than the second one. I will therefore begin by briefly discussing the first.

You may have heard about one the core texts of Tibetan Buddhism, called *Bardo Thodol*, a title often translated in English as *The Tibetan Book of the Dead*. This very important piece of spiritual literature is in many ways no different to what I am attempting to do here. Obviously, I don't even dream to compare my work with profound wisdom more than a thousand years old, but it is true that, in substance, the *Bardo Thodol* is a description of the death process and of what happens after the transition. Taking into account the differences in language and style, the similarities with what reported by NDErs and spirit communicators in modern times are both substantial and striking.

A point that Tibetan Buddhism makes very clear is that the state of mind in which one passes over has a major impact on the process of dying, and especially on how the early stages of life in the spirit world are experienced. Dying suddenly, unprepared, may in some cases result in negative, unpleasant experiences immediately after the passing. This may include temporarily finding oneself in a dark or hazy, lonely, barren place and experiencing disorientation and possibly fear. These experiences are generally of short duration, but it goes without saying that they would better be avoided. In other cases, as we will shortly see from testimony, dying in great suffering and, particularly, in psychological turmoil may require those newly arrived into the spirit world to go through a period compared to deep sleep, often referred to as "second death", explained as rest and recuperation and preparation for the following stages of life in the spirit world.

Very interestingly, a medieval prayer from Christian Europe asks God for deliverance from various evils and dangers including "...and sudden death". Similar problems of fear and confusion possibly following a sudden, unprepared death are also stressed in non-Christian traditions such as shamanic religions in Native America and Asia. Essentially, what we learn from these old teachings is that if one is in a state of fear, anger, bitterness, or distracted by material concerns or attachment to worldly goods, the result can be a confused and disturbing entry into the next world. Conversely, a tranquil and fully accepting mind at the moment of death is capable of experiencing a peaceful transition into the next world, essential if one is to remain properly aware of what is happening and to have some control over the immediate afterlife state. Time and again, we are told that being prepared – as in having a good general understanding of what the process is like on both sides of death – is the best guarantee for a positive experience. I therefore like to think that, by reading this book and reflecting on its content and key messages, you are essentially buying a ticket to a good early afterlife!

This point is put forward in no uncertain terms by "Scott" one of the spirit communicators coming through Jane Sherwood, a serious, gifted non-professional medium:

> "I think the experience of death must vary considerably because it is governed by the state of mind in which one passes over. Also there is a vast difference between a sudden passing and a quiet and prepared one. The shock of an unnatural death sets the being in mad turmoil. One finds oneself in a fantastic dream world with no continuity of experience … the chaos of unconnected states of mind have no proper framework of space and time… Much of this earlier nightmare could be avoided in one knows how to avail himself of the help that is offered."

Now, coming to the second, larger and deeper concept of souls possessing varying degrees of age and experience, I may be getting a little ahead of myself. This is indeed a key concept, one which we will examine in depth in the later chapter describing what we learn about what I would call the overall scheme of life, including in the material and spirit worlds. This, as we will see, includes multiple incarnations in the physical realm, essentially serving the purpose of making experiences, learning lessons and progressing towards higher levels of consciousness. Without going into any detail now, I think it's not difficult to appreciate how an "older", "more developed" soul possessing a higher, finer, more spiritual and less materialistic mind and consciousness is likely to have a comparatively easier transition into the early afterlife.

A peaceful transition

Judging by reports of NDErs and by communications through mediums, those who die peacefully and reasonably prepared typically are aware of making a journey, often through darkness or a tunnel and often towards a distant bright light. Spirit communicators speak of a sensation of weightlessness and of great freedom, with an absence of physical pain or the disabilities they may have been experiencing before leaving their body. There is rarely any talk of fear for what lies ahead, or regret and longing for what was left behind. Often there is a feeling of being loved and cared for, either by the spirit helpers who may have come forward to greet the newly deceased or by some unseen force connected with the bright light.

The same Mike Swain we encountered before, communicated to his father that he immediately found his Uncle Mark standing beside him:

> "He explained that ... we were no longer in the land of the living. I was too surprised to ask him how he knew, although I did have a hunch I was dead, and it seemed perfectly natural that he had come to take charge of me. I can't say exactly how long it took for me to leave the earth plane. It was rather much like flipping a radio dial from one station to another. When you turn the knob, you take for granted that another station will be awaiting your pleasure, you don't think there is anything unusual about it. That's how I moved from your world to my new one. All our family, even the ones I didn't know when I was on earth, where there to welcome me. They made me feel wanted and very much at home."

William T. Stead, a spiritualist and therefore fully knowledgeable about the afterlife perspective, was a victim of the 1912 *Titanic* disaster. Communicating through his daughter Estelle, Stead recall that his first awareness that he had passed over was when he found himself surrounded by deceased relatives:

> "I knew at once, and I was a trifle alarmed. Practically instantaneously I found myself looking for myself. Just a moment of agitation, momentarily only, and then the

full and glorious realisation that all I had learnt *was* true."

The noted psychical researcher Rev Drayton Thomas mentions a communication received through a medium from one Colonel Cosgrove:

"I remember feeling rather peculiar, I suppose it would be the night before I passed over. I did not think I was going, but felt less clear in mind than usual. About dawn, I had a sinking feeling, and the daylight seemed to go. I seemed to be swaying about in the dark and felt slightly giddy. Then the atmosphere seemed to become light around me and I heard voices, but they were not the voices of the people on earth, they were the voices of my two dear boys, the voices I had not heard for many long years. I did not feel impatient, I knew they were there and that I should not lose them again. I was content to wait until I should be able to speak to them. I did not feel that wild joy, that great elation, that I had always expected to feel. I was not in the state for it, but felt heavy, stupid and sleepy, yet at peace and full of confidence and quiet happiness knowing they were round me. Now and again I heard other voices, but they seemed far away. I suppose those were the voices of people actually in the room with me. He nearer vocies were those of my boys."

As I mentioned earlier, others, particularly those who have long been ill, drift in and out of consciousness; their re-adjustment to the new world is gradual and often punctuated by sleep. Such sleep, which for some is perceived as quite long, is often called "second death". This is always described as a welcome, regenerating rest, one that prepares the newly arrived for more wondrous experiences that await.

In a script received through automatic writing by Zoe Richmond in the UK, her brother Joe says:

"The spirit longs to rest, there comes the great desire to sleep. In that sleep a great deal happens, but I don't yet know enough to tell you about it. It is not exactly a sleep, but your sleep in the earthly life is pretty much the nearest thing to it ... All you know is that you wake up another being. When the spirit comes out of that sleep he knows where he is and what he is, as you sometimes wake up in the morning with some knotty problem solved.

Those who pass over with a full knowledge and understanding of the life beyond do not need that sleep at all, unless they come over with their spirit tired by a long illness or the worries of life. In practice almost everyone needs the sleep period for a shorter or longer time. The greater the difficulty of the spirit in adjusting himself to the new conditions, the longer and deeper the sleep period that is necessary."

And the Colonel Cosgrove we quoted above says:

"After a time of unconsciousness, I seemed to have become clearer quite suddenly. It was like a burst of sunshine, and I looked. I seemed able to move my eyes quite suddenly, and in the burst of sight and light I saw my boys, my brothers, and many others around me."

A less peaceful transition

The early afterlife following a sudden, traumatic, unexpected death, especially for someone who is not familiar with the concept of an afterlife, can be an uneasy – and occasionally harrowing – affair. A spirit identifying himself as Thomas Dowding, a schoolmaster who joined the British army and was killed on the battlefield in World War I, communicated to Wellesley Tudor Pole that one moment he was alive and the next he was helping two of his friends carry his body down the trench labyrinth.

> "I didn't know whether I had jumped out of my body through shell shock, temporarily or forever. You see what a small thing death is, even the violent death of war! I seemed in a dream... Death for me was a simple experience – no horror, no long drawn suffering, no conflict. It comes to many in the same way."

Dowdling said he experienced no pain when struck by a shell splinter. After his body was taken to the filed mortuary, he remained near it for the whole night, expecting to wake up in the body again. He then lost consciousness. When he awoke the next morning, his body was gone and he began hunting for it. He then realised that he must be dead. Once he recovered from the shock of the realisation, he felt as he were floating in a mist that muffled sound and blurred the vision.

> "It was like looking through the wrong end of a telescope. Everything was distant, minute, misty, unreal. Guns were being fired. It might all have been millions of miles away... I think I fell asleep for a second time, and long remained asleep in a dreamless state. When I awoke, I think my new faculties were in working order. I can reason, and think, and feel and move."

You can see from this account as those unprepared for death may straddle the two worlds for some time, receiving sensory inputs from both and in fact believing themselves to still be on the earthly plane. The same, as I had hinted before, may happen to those who have a strong attachment to earthly life, including material possessions. This can create confusion, anxiety, and may delay the transition to the next stages of the afterlife. In such cases, the recently departed may experience a place of haunting shadows, or regrets and unfulfilled longings, of aching loneliness, of sadness for lost opportunities, and a remorse for the suffering one may have caused in life. One of medium's Jane Sherwood communicators says:

> "I spent a long sojourn in what I think of as Hades, the place of the shade, a dim and formless world which I

believe is peopled by the miasma of earth emotions and the unconscious projections of its inhabitants…"

However, save exceptional cases which are beyond the scope of this book, permanence in this confused and confounding, unpleasant dimension is temporary. Albert Pauchard, founder and President of the Geneva Metaphysical Society, communicated after death through a non-professional medium that after his first feelings of bliss at his "liberation" he found himself in a dark region where he walked along a seemingly endless road and was aware at some point that "…there was no sky … no perspective … no depth … no free space … There was nothing. I was alone in a desolating place." However, when in due course Pauchard emerged from this state, spirit helpers informed him it represented "all depressions and despondencies" he had experienced while on earth, and he happily progressed towards the next stages of the afterlife experience.

Chapter ten

The life review

The key concept that relates to and in some way captures the essence of the next stage of life in the spirit world is simple, uplifting and a further reason for great hope.

> *In the afterlife we are not judged and absolved or condemned – there are no judges and there is no eternal damnation. We are simply helped to reflect and learn from our earthly passage. This can be a painful experience, but is fundamental for our growth.*

It is interesting to note how this concept is in direct contradiction to what a large proportion of the people of faith believe, and yet NDErs and spirit communicators have expressed it with incredible consistency, often using very similar words, regardless of the period when the testimony was provided, the country, the social, economic, cultural and religious background of the witnesses. Although, as ever, details of the experience vary to some extent – particularly concerning the modality of the life review – the key concept I introduced above is always very powerfully put forward.

The amount of precise, explicit testimony on this particular stage is such that I will now let our witnesses entirely do the job of explaining. We begin with a selection of brief quotes from NDErs:

> "The life review was absolutely, positively, everything for the first 33 years of my life… from the first breath of life right through the accident."

> "It proceeded to show me every single event in my life, in a kind of instant three-dimensional panoramic

review… The brightness showed me every second of all those years, in exquisite detail, in what seemed only an instant of time."

"My whole life was there, every instant of it… Everyone and everything I had ever seen and everything that had ever happened was there. "

"Then I was seeing my whole life from beginning to end, even all those little things you forget along the way."

"I had a total, complete, clear knowledge of everything that had ever happened in my life – even little minute things I had forgotten."

"My life passed before me… even things I had forgotten all about. Every single emotion, all the happy times, the sad times, the angry times, the love, the reconciliation – everything was there. Nothing was left out."

According to NDErs testimony, the life review often takes the shape of a judgment process that the spirit carries out on his/her own, or with the help and assistance of other beings:

"You are shown your life – and you do the judging."

"I was asked what had I done to benefit or advance the human race. At the same time, all my life was present instantly in front of me and I was shown or made to understand what counted."

"[the Being of Light's] love encouraged me to go through my life up to that point. I saw, relived, remembered things that has happened in my life; not only what actually took place, but the emotions involved. […] I could see for myself and with open eyes and without defences what actions of mine had caused pain."

"Mine was not a review but a reliving. For me, it was a total reliving of every thought I had ever thought, every word I had ever spoken, and every deed I had ever done; plus the effect of each thought, word and deed on everyone and anyone who had ever come within my environment or sphere of influence, whether I knew them or not."

"[A prisoner found that a scroll began to unroll before his vision and comments:] And the only pictures on it were the pictures of the people I had injured. There would be no end to it. A vast number of those people I knew or had seen. Then there were hundreds I had never seen. These were people who had been indirectly injured by me. The minute history of my long criminal career was thus relived by me, plus all the small injuries I had inflicted unconsciously. Apparently nothing was omitted in this nightmare of injuries, but the most terrifying thing about it was that every pang of suffering I had caused to others was now felt by me as the scroll unwound itself."

Total agreement between NDErs and spirit communicators

So much for NDErs, but what do people who have actually died have to say? I've come across dozens of quotes from spirit communicators using almost the same words to describe the same process. For instance, in Naples, Italy, Professor Giorgio di Simone of the Italian Parapsychology Society collected and analysed for over thirty years the recordings of the extraordinary direct voice mediumship of a local medium. Incidentally, some of these recordings were studied by the Electro Acoustics Department of Turin University and compared with recordings of the same sentences pronounced by the medium when not in trance. The conclusion of the laboratory was that "the voices are produced by different individuals". Concerning the life review process, the communicating entity said:

> "The dead person 'dreams' all his life, is confronted with all the deeds he did and can take stock exactly of the good or evil, of whether his life was useful or useless. He can weigh each individual deed, linking that to the overall evolution of his soul. Contrary to what it is believed on earth, it is not God passing the judgment, God is not the judge! The judge of the soul is the soul itself."

And from further north in Italy, Florence, where striking materializations and direct voice phenomena characterized for three decades the séances of medium Roberto Setti before he prematurely died in 1984, we learn from one of the communicators:

> "When the individual has ceased to exist, he abandons the physical body but remains nearby it for some time and is greatly disturbed by the distress of those left behind. He then goes through a life review and is often helped in this first contact with the spiritual world by people who died before him. [...] Souls painfully relive their misdeeds, and, as a consequence, are purified."

In Paris, France, circa 1860, entity George communicating through the automatic writing of medium Madame Costel said that:

> "Then, the memory of the life he [the deceased] has left behind appears with enormous clarity. This is an experience at times devastating, at times exhilarating, at times consoling. All prejudices are dropped, truth appears in all its brightness and one's soul is seen like in a mirror".

Jane Sherwood, a British automatic writing medium, received messages from a spirit referred to as E.K. This is how he describes the life review:

"It raced over the record of a long lifetime which it lit up with a searchlight that spared no blunders, sins or weaknesses, but impartially illuminated it all, as one holds up an old, finished garment to the light and notes with dismay its rents and stains. This clear breeze of recollection showed me the honest cut and shape of the thing too. I reviewed it as though I had no longer a special responsibility for it but had to understand clearly in what it had failed and in what it had succeeded."

The spirit communicators often speak of the difficulty of translating into earthly language an experience which, like all others in the spirit world, is perfectly understandable to them but basically ineffable for us. Communicating through the hand of Mrs E.B. Duffey, a "dear friend" of hers put it this way:

"How can I describe to you which has no parallel on earth? I can give you an imperfect idea of what occurred, although it came to me with a force that I had never experienced either in my earthly life or in my spiritual existence. The air seemed filled with a strange murmur, and clouds descended and shut from my view all outwards objects ... The story of my life was being told in tones that, it seemed to me, must reach to the farthest heavens, and its events were pictured before me by the tossing clouds. I use the words heard and saw, and yet I am not sure that I did either. But the impression made upon my mind was if all senses had united in one grand effort to place my past life in its true phases before me. I sat appalled and dismayed, and then the record of weaknesses and failures went on, I covered my face with hands and sank in agony and shame to the ground ... I summoned all my courage, and since I must sit in judgment on myself, I resolved to do this bravely and thoroughly. How many sombre pictures were there! How many half light, half shade; but now and then there was a bright one in which some unconscious unselfishness, some little deed I had done and forgotten, without any thought of secret self-glorification, and which had not only been good in its results, but which had sprung from a fountain of genuine good within my heart, shone out like a jewel from the dark clouds which surrounded it."

As you can see, dear reader, every experience is unique and the ways to describe it are as many as those who have it. However, I hope that this selection of accounts spanning several continents and different periods in modern history will convince you that the *nature* of the experience of the life review is absolutely the same for everybody.

Chapter eleven
The illusion of Summerland

It is now time for me to introduce what I consider as possibly the most difficult among the key concepts that open each chapter dedicated to a stage of life in the spirit world. When I say difficult, I do not necessarily mean difficult to understand – I would rather say, for some people, difficult to accept.

The first proper, full encounter with life in the spirit world happens in an environment which is perceived as absolutely real, but in fact is created by, and responds to, the soul's thoughts.

Please remember that, for lack of a better word, I call "soul" the discarnate personality who has recently shed his or her physical body and, at the current stage of the process, has possibly gone through periods of restorative "sleep" and, almost certainly, has experienced a life review. At this point, the soul enters an environment which – essentially – we could call heaven. Some authors have called it Summerland, and I borrowed this definition, for it very well corresponds to the kind of experiences the soul has there. Incidentally, as we will see, NDErs too have very similar experiences whilst clinically dead and therefore without a functioning brain.

Adding "illusion" to the definition of Summerland may seem to diminish it, but in fact it does not. Although well beyond the scope of this book, you may want to remember that, according to the conclusions of several branches of science, including neurophysiology, psychology and, most importantly, modern physics, we too, here on earth, in the material world, live in a reality which is essentially an illusion. Our conscious perception of the world *does not* correspond to how the world is in reality – it is the product of an extraordinary work of selection and recombination of sensory stimuli, carried out by our brain with the aim of making us most fit to survive in our environment. Plenty of popular science books have been written about this subject, and if you want to deepen your understanding of this counter-intuitive idea you will find a few good recommendations in the references section.

So, I would ask, why should an environment in which we exist as pure consciousness, mind and personality be any different? The important thing is that, just like the illusion we live here on earth, the illusion of Summerland appears absolutely real and material to the souls. With one key difference, though: since Summerland is created by our thoughts, it *responds* to thoughts too. In technical words, we describe this feature as *psychoplasticity*, i.e. the capacity of the mind to mould what appears as a real, material world. Before we move any further, let me bring in a spirit communicator to drive this concept home.

During the first two decades of the 20th century, English medium Ernest H. Peckham received several messages from a spirit, reverend A. H. Stockwell, who had died 40 years earlier. Stockwell provided several details about his life, which Peckham and his group researched and found correct, and said that his mission in the afterlife consisted precisely in communicating to the living information about the afterlife. Rev Stockwell says:

> "Let me say that there are no two disincarnate personalities who live the same experience. […] I, for instance, started feeling a need for company; as that feeling grew inside me, I saw the environment around me transforming, expanding, and becoming more beautiful than ever. Then, I started seeing spiritual beings coming towards me from all sides in jubilation. I was to learn afterwards that that miracle was due to my desire for a 'psychic rapport' between me and the other beings on the same spiritual plane."

A place all of us very much would wish to visit

No surprise, therefore, that life in Summerland pretty much resembles life on earth. The souls – whether of deceased individuals or of people who have temporarily crossed the threshold in a near-death experience – have only recently left their worldly life, and naturally tend to re-create a familiar environment. Only, because of the nature of the non-physical reality where souls exist and how this reality responds to thoughts, its features are nothing short of marvellous and stunning. Let's begin with some testimony from NDErs:

> "I could see a marvellous landscape, a sort of park with extraordinarily bright colours, and in particular an emerald-green lawn with the grass cut short. It was Spring and the lawn was full of small multicoloured flowers I had never seen before. The area was bathed in very bright sunlight, and the colours were of an indescribable splendour. The slope was bordered with trees of a darker green."

> "My spirit was wandering in a landscape which might have been painted by Walt Disney. Very green fields, of a tender emerald colour, big leafy trees, enormous, colourful flowers."

> "Meanwhile, I was immersed in music that seemed to come out of a sound system in four, five, six dimensions. The sun was pulsating, and I knew that the sun was the divine principle, the alpha and the omega, the source of all energies and all manifestations. What I was seeing was not the sun, but a wonderful apparition similar to the sun - warm, bright. My soul was vibrating in harmony with the vibrations of that sun, and I felt more and more happy and at ease."

And now, let's see what the dead have to tell us. We begin with William Stead, a British journalist who was among the victims of the sinking of the Titanic in 1912. Within minutes of the tragedy, Stead's daughter received a message from her father through automatic writing, in which he announced he was dead and he indicated the exact time at which the transatlantic ship had collided with the iceberg. This, to the young lady's complete shock, happened before any information was communicated by radio and newspapers in the UK. In later communications, Stead, who was keen not to talk about his death but rather to describe his experience of the afterlife, said:

> "The arrival was marvellous. It was like coming out of a foggy and dark English landscape to find ourselves all of a sudden under the blue Indian sky. Everything was beauty and splendour. We knew that we were approaching the place where these souls, suddenly taken away from earthly life, would find their first home. Something that really surprised me was the colour of the surrounding landscape. It was pale blue, with different shades. I don't mean that everything – trees, houses, people – was blue, but the overall impression was of that colour. Light itself contained an intense blue radiation."

And in the early 1960s, in France, a deceased young man so describes his experience to his mother through the words of a medium:

> "Think of everything we consider magic or enchanting in nature on earth, like water, stars, shells, fireflies and the singing of birds – that is only a pale reflection of our kingdom. Do you remember how I showed an early taste for beauty? It was just an intuition of what was to come. Here everything is shrouded in stars, covered in flowers, scents abound; imagine extraordinary vegetation."

Going back for a moment to Rev Stockwell, here is how he describes Summerland:

> "Hearing is such a poor vehicle to channel impressions when compared to seeing. How can one describe the beauty of a sunrise on the Swiss Alps, with its

shimmering glory of multiple golden shades, using the chords of a musical instrument? And, how could I accurately and adequately describe to you the glory of spiritual existence using the raw language of the living? The landscape that opened up in front of me was of an incomparable beauty and seemed to expand infinitely in all directions. Above it, a blue sky of a mesmerizing beauty. But the most extraordinary feature of this landscape was that distant objects did not at all appear smaller in size as would be the case on earth. Perspective was literally transformed. And that's not all; as I realized that I could visually perceive objects from all sides at one time and not just from the one visible side as happens in the world of the living. This enhanced, expanded vision produces wondrous effects. When you look at the outer surface of whatever object, you can actually see inside it, around it and through it, because spiritual vision allows you to penetrate the object of observation in its entirety."

Very interestingly, this quote about the enhanced vision has brought to my mind many several similar ones from people describing Out of Body Experiences in the 1970s and 1980s, such as this one:

"Few objects are visible, but I feel intense energy radiating around me. As I look around, I realize that I don't need to turn my head; I seem to see wherever I direct my thoughts, and I can see in every direction simultaneously; I'm a 360-degree viewpoint without form or substance."

The power of thoughts and desires

So, even from these few accounts we can see that NDErs and spirit communicators use broadly similar words to describe a broadly similar experience in the "psychoplastic" environment moulded by and responsive to thoughts and desires. We hear general descriptions of fantastic landscapes, shimmering colours, and – especially – of bright light and warmth associated with an unequivocal feeling of cosmic love. And yet, communicators insist on the very particular nature of the environment where they find themselves at this stage:

> "Ours is a world of thought and everything in it is a creation of thought. Around us creations of our thoughts take form to mingle and harmonize with the creations of other souls' thoughts. Naturally, it is difficult for anybody living on earth to understand this, and still these are simple processes, natural and amazingly effective."

Contributing to the sense of absolute reality of this experience is the fact that the creative power of thoughts and desires is not unlimited:

> "There are things ... as the same kind as you see on earth, only somehow different. They are real, but you have a sense that they are only temporary, that they belong to that particular stage.
>
> Then you find, and it seems very curious and fascinating, that you can change those things by wishing them to change. You can only do it with small and unimportant things ... you can't change big things, you can't change the whole scene around you. That is because it is not only your scene, it belongs to lots of other spirits too, but you can change any little thing, when the change won't affect anybody else. He you begin to realise that all the things around you are really thought forms, and that it is arranged like that in order to make the transition easy from material life to spirit life."

And, there are further mentions of the fact that the kind of life one has lived on earth, the stage of evolution of a particular soul, contribute to shaping the stage in the afterlife we have called Summerland:

"So, where does the soul find itself? It is immersed in that particular state of existence that its mental, moral, spiritual condition make possible for it. The environment which welcomes it is determined by the degree of spirituality in which the soul finds itself. Through death, it reaches that spiritual sojourn that it has prepared for itself, and it can't go anywhere else. [...] The future residence is already contained in the soul itself and its spiritual companions are the beings similar to it."

Life in Summerland

Now, I am sure you, the reader, will be wanting to know more about what it is like to experience life in Summerland. What do discarnate personalities *do?* How do they *live?* And *where?* These are of course legitimate questions, and they are also relevant, at least for the stage in the afterlife experience we called Summerland. As I have already said, Summerland comes early, when the soul still has strong memories and imprints from the earthly life, and therefore many features of this environment closely resemble life on Earth. In fact, we should say an idealised form of life on Earth.

Why and how this is so is beautifully explained in a communication received by F.W.H. Myers, the Cambridge academic who was among the founders of the Society for Psychical Research:

"Nearly every soul lives for a time in the state of illusion. The vast majority of human beings when they die are dominated by the conception that substance is the only reality. They are not prepared for a complete and sudden change of outlook. They passionately yearn for familiar though idealised surroundings. Their will to live is merely to live, therefore, in the past. So they enter that dream I call illusion-land. For instance, Tom Jones, who represents the unthinking man in the street, will desire a glorified brick villa in a glorified Brighton ... He

> naturally gravitates towards his acquaintances, all those who were of a like mind ... But he is merely dreaming all the time, or, rather, living within the fantasy created by his strongest desires on earth"

Logically, then, the body spirits perceive themselves as having resembles the body they had when they were at peak form in their lives. If you had to imagine a body for yourself, after all, wouldn't you like to have the body you had when you were 25? Very interestingly, in many apparitional cases the deceased person reportedly appears with a younger body, sometimes strikingly lacking disabilities that had occurred at later stages in life. This would suggest that when spirits "project" themselves into the material world (or, possibly, when people on earth are temporarily allowed perceptions of the spirit world) the body is the same idealised version of the body experienced by souls in Summerland. Anyhow, we should concede that we will never understand, or be able to imagine, what exactly souls at this particular stage experience as their own body.

T.E. Lawrence, communicating through a medium, says:

> "I still miss the weight of my earth body, I suppose, although I should be sorry now to have to drag it about ... my present body, solid as it seems, is now really composed of a kind of matter which on earth I thought of as 'emotion'. This 'feeling stuff' is now exterior to the real me and has no physical drag to slow down its activity."

A beautiful description of life in Summerland comes from the Albert Pauchard we already quoted earlier, saying to his daughter through a medium:

> "Remarkable is the impression of *time*, which is not measured in the same way as on earth. Thus it seemed to me that I had spent at least several months in the 'Elysian Fields' – or what I took for them. I was in a state of serene bliss, of complete relaxation.

In the beginning, I was more or less conscious of the presence of loved and family faces ... it seemed to me, as though all around me were large and fresh fields covered with flowers. I was constantly surrounded by this golden haze. But I rather felt things rather than saw them ... I saw a great many things that were new to me. I walked about, I met many an old friend and some new ones. So that I had the impression of having lived here for a long time.

When my attention turned towards you again, I realised that *this lapse of time, so long and full, corresponded to three or four terrestrial days."*

This particular testimony reminds us of another critical aspect of existence in the early stages of the afterlife: from there, spirits *remain aware* of what happens in the lives of their loved ones on earth. For reasons that, yet again, we do not begin to understand, souls in the spirit world have comparatively much less difficulty in being aware of the earthly world they have left behind, whilst contacts with the spirit world are rare for ordinary people on earth, and possible for a small minority of gifted mediums.

Time to move on

In the first long quote of the next chapter, we will have a chance to learn more about how souls spend their "time" in this blissful, idealised, heavenly reality. Now we have to understand that, following a natural, organic process – one that evolves differently for different souls, for some very slowly, for others very rapidly – there is an irresistible drive to soar toward higher, more spiritual, less material-looking dimensions.

In his book *Living On*, author Paul Beard, who has thoroughly researched the records of thousands of spirit communications on the subject of life in the spirit world, writes:

So in the end the self-created enjoyments which he has been creating lose their meaning and savour. What at first seemed so desirable and satisfying (and of which meanwhile he may have given descriptions to friends on earth through a medium) now proves to be an illusion. A sense of stagnation descends upon him, he tires of his own felicity, for something is stirring within him which tells him he is not satisfied, that there are hidden areas of life ahead of him. Once the traveller accepts that these pleasures have no further meaning for him, he becomes willing to let them go.

A spirit communicator, however, reassures us that:

> "You will find that the gratification of your desires quickly palls, but at least you have the pleasure of it before this happens ... No, it does not last. It is not meant to. But you will have it as long as you want. Nobody will hurry you ... You yourself will be sated with it first."

Chapter twelve
The first heaven

The key concept I would like to introduce now is self-evident when reflecting on what we have learnt so far. Still, it is so fundamentally important that it is essential to spell it out here.

The spirit world is organised in different "levels", from the "lower" ones, closer to the material world, to progressively "higher" ones, closer to the pure consciousness (you can call it God if you are a religious person) which is the ultimate nature of all that exists.

In fact, a more correct formulation would say that life itself, whether in the material or in the nonmaterial spirit world is organised in levels, or layers. The life we live on Earth, then, is life at the lowest, more "dense", more material and less spiritual of these levels. This is very, very important, because it helps us understand how there is no substantial difference between our earthly experience and the experiences that await us after shedding the material body: on Earth, we are consciousness with a material body, in spirit we are consciousness with a mental body, at first, and then gradually move towards consciousness. But consciousness we were, we are, and we'll always be.

In order to illustrate this "nesting" of different levels, let me quote a very high-level testimony, received from an evidently very advanced, enlightened soul communicating via the direct voices method for more than 25 years (between the 1960s and the mid-1980s) through the extraordinary mediumship of Roberto Setti in Florence, Italy. Setti, an insurance broker by profession, was an absolutely ordinary person, a quiet, somewhat shy family man, who nevertheless showed superstar mediumistic qualities, gathering a small following of researchers and scholars around him who, séance after séance, year after year, painstakingly recorded and transcribed everything that was uttered by these mysterious voices, appearing independently, all with their own tone and mannerism, as speaking out of thin air in different points of the séance room. These voices were recorded on tape, and their messages carefully transcribed. Much of this material has been published over the years, but it is unfortunately only available in the original Italian language.

As we explore what this evolved soul has to say, please remember that the terminology used (physical plane, astral plane, akashic plan, etc) is often found in testimony from spirit communicators, but we should not get hung-up on it. Other terminologies have been used by others, and we should take all of these terms as just an attempt to communicate concepts. The spirit world, alas, is far from an exact science.

> "The environment in which the individual evolves is composed of the physical plane, the astral plane, the mental plane, the akashic plane and the spiritual planes.
>
> All planes of existence are around you: the world of spirits is within matter itself. But man, when incarnated, cannot perceive more than what his restricted physical senses allow. For every field of existence, the individual has different vehicles or bodies; the astral body is concerned with emotional life, sensations, desires; the mental body gives man all the faculties which are typical of the mind, intellect and thoughts; the akashic body or consciousness receives and transcribes the reality that man discovers and acquires through existence, transforming it in the very nature of the individual.
>
> When the individual has ceased to exist, he abandons the physical body but remains nearby it for some time and is greatly disturbed by the distress of those left behind. He then goes through a life review and is often helped in this first contact with the spiritual world by people who died before him.

The astral world is very similar to the physical world: a very vast and wonderful world inhabited by a great multitude of individuals. The length of time souls spend at this level depends on the degree of spiritual evolution they have reached: evolved souls remain for just a short while, whilst less evolved souls create a virtual world for themselves which enables them to tend to unfulfilled desires; and this until, tired and satisfied, a soul finds itself on the threshold of the next plane, the mental plane, the existence of which it hadn't even imagined until then.

In the mental plane, every creature is immersed in continuous meditation and contemplates experiences of the last incarnation: scientists keep on studying those problems they were not able to solve, so that in the next incarnation they will carry the solutions within themselves. Once all the material accumulated during the last incarnation has been worked through, the individual leaves the mental plane and the faculties he has acquired there are fed into the akashic plane that is the individual's consciousness.

The akashic body retains the imprint of all the experiences lived during the various incarnations and gradually takes shape as the individual evolves. If the individual is not highly evolved, the akashic body is not sufficiently formed and therefore remains on this plane, quietly reviewing all past existences until it is ready for a new incarnation which will further expand his consciousness. If, on the contrary, the akashic body is sufficiently formed, the individual lives a lucid existence centered on the noble sentiments deriving from his acquired consciousness. From this plane of existence he radiates boundless love and limitless compassion towards others.

This is therefore the plane of universal brotherhood and love: the plane where you all will live consciously, understanding that all the difficulties that trouble you now are experiences necessary for your evolution, for your spiritual rebirth. When the individual feels he is at one with the rest of creation, he leaves the akashic plane, getting closer to the very centre of his being, to the divine light, and is ready to reach the spiritual planes and conquer the cosmic, absolute consciousness.

It is very difficult to talk to you, who are living in matter, about spiritual planes; knowing about their existence, however, makes them more easily reachable."

Like Summerland, only better

If we look at the communication quoted above, it is evident that what we called Summerland corresponds to the "astral plane", and what we are going to describe in this chapter is the "mental plane". Admittedly, what we call First Heaven is not overly different from Summerland. My personal opinion is that this essentially is a "better defined" Summerland. At this stage, the soul has rested enough and has had time to adapt to the new spiritual dimension, so it is time to reflect, consolidate the learning received during the recent earthly life and, for many, to remain engaged in the same activities that were important for them in the material world. This happens for the purpose of the soul's growth, rather than for pure satisfaction of essential but general and vague desires and wishes as it happened in Summerland. The environment in the First Heaven, still entirely created by the interaction between the thoughts of all individual souls, is considerably more complex and in many ways even more like an idealised version of earthly life. The traveller is now placed in a place of intensified perception and of deepened emotional relationships.

F.W.H. Myers communicates:

"You dwell in a world which is the original of the earth. Briefly, the earth is an ugly, smudged copy of the world wherein dwells the subtle soul in its subtle body."

Interestingly, exactly the same concept appears in a totally independent communication by W.T. Stead:

"This world which I have been in for a long time now, is the closest thing imaginable to your earth ... You will say, 'Oh, then it is only a reflection of our world'. It is not that way – the earth is only a reflection of *this* world. Earth is not the lasting world. It's the training school."

A spirit called Henry, who, communicating through Gordon Phinn, described himself as "a boring accountant", speaks of the physical surroundings and of activities:

"The city shines ahead, as all cities do on this level. When you first arrive, fresh from the land of old age and winter gloom, you think it's the building that are shining. Then you refine that to, no, they're emitting light, they're glowing. Then you see the people are too. And the trees. And the flowers. And the rivers. Then you realise that it comes with the territory. When you exist on this level, you shine. And then, after a while, you get used to it and you don't notice any more.

I think you've realised by now there are very few vehicles here. People stroll, float, or think themselves to places. Vehicles are still maintained by those who love the thought of them. Vintage car lovers have their rallies here just as they did on earth. Horse and buggy fanciers do the same. Skiers ski in the mountains; water skiers do the same on lakes.

But nobody *needs* these methods of transport, They're much loved habits extended for fun. As one set of dead people grows out of their earth-bound ways and look for more refined applications of their ever-expanding talents, another set appears to take up the slack. As on earth, the graduating class always has its replacements."

Gordon Burdick told medium Grace Rosher that the reality on his side was much like what he had experienced when alive in the flesh:

> "Life here is in a sense a continuation of our existence on earth, and not of an unfamiliar kind. We have work to do. It's not just one long holiday. We live under conditions much like those on earth. We have homes, there are places of entertainment and of learning. The children are brought up in very much the same way as in the old world."

In terms of activities, when Alice Gilbert asked her deceased son Philip about carrying over one's interests in such things as art, music and cricket to the afterlife, Philip gave a "yes and no" answer, telling her it was very difficult to explain.

> "If anyone has got anything on his mind, an obsession for, say, cricket, he will live in an illusion world of that, and will not attain his full power of knowledge of how to get on here till he has snapped out of it and that may take centuries [in Earth time]. Any activity which depends for its impetus on physical body skill such as sport, or even investing in the stock market has no equivalent in the reality here. However, such activities such as music, art, and mathematics can be continued here as they are universal activities that extend from the afterlife realm to earth."

The already cited Rev Stockwell says:

> "It is not possible to give a comprehensive and exhaustive idea of the extraordinary diverse range of occupations and spiritual activities ... In any case, these activities greatly transcend the earthly ones in their scope, kind, in their potential, in their effects, in their usefulness, stability, beauty and grandiosity. Ours are

> purely spiritual activities, for spiritual aims and carried out through spiritual agents, of which you naturally know nothing, or very little ... Ours is a world of thought and everything in it is a substantive creation of thought. All around us, the creations of our thoughts take form, and they fuse and harmonise with the creations of the thoughts of others. Naturally, for those in an earthly environment it is difficult to understand, and yet these are simple and natural processes and stunningly effective."

Interestingly, and I, for one, cannot really think of a reason why it should be this way, we have few accounts of the First Heaven by NDErs. It would appear that, in their brief foray into the spirit world, NDErs "skip" this particular level. As we have seen, following an NDE we have plenty of accounts of the "lower" realms, and, as we will see in the following chapters, we also have pretty good testimony about the "higher" spheres. However, precious little is said about the abode we called First Heaven. By scanning my bookshelves, I was only able to find one, partly fitting, report:

> "I arrived at a place - it's very hard to put this into words - I can only describe it as Heaven. It's a place of intense light, a place of intense activity, more like a bustling city than a lonely country scene, nothing like floating on clouds, harps or anything of that sort. While I was there I felt at the centre of things. I felt enlightened and cleansed. I felt I could see the point of everything. Everything fitted in, it all made sense, even the dark times. It almost seemed, too, as if the pieces of a jig-saw all fitted together."

We end up where we belong

The concept of training school mentioned in Rev Stockwell's quote above is important, and worth dwelling on for a bit, for we have been clearly and repeatedly told that the kind of life we lived on earth (corresponding to the level of development or "age" of our soul, as we discussed earlier) has a direct influence on the conditions we find ourselves in the first heaven.

This is well explained by Robert Hare Sr., a prominent Philadelphia merchant and politician, communicating with his son through a device called *spiritoscope*, which Robert Jr., a renowned inventor and professor emeritus of chemistry at the university of Pennsylvania, had built to facilitate communication with the spirit world. Robert Sr. says:

> "The spirit goes to a sphere for which it is morally and intellectually adapted. Each sphere is divided into six circles, or societies, in which congenial spirits are united and subsist together according to the law of affinity. While these spirits generally agree in moral and intellectual matters, there are individual differences and some disagreements. Spirits united by ties of consanguinity may or may not be linked together in the spheres and in the same society. It depends on the affinity between them, including the level of advancement. However, a spirit in a higher sphere can pass to a lower one to visit loved ones. But a spirit can never ascend to the higher spheres until fully prepared for such transition.
>
> Each society has teachers from those above, as well as from higher spheres, whose duty is to impart knowledge acquired from their instructions and experiences. Thus, by receiving and giving knowledge our moral and intellectual faculties are expanded to higher conceptions and more exalted view of the great Creator."

Rev Stockwell, again communicating through Ernest H. Peckham, says:

> "Where therefore the newly born spirit finds itself? He is immersed in that state of existence which his mental, moral and spiritual conditions make the only one

possible for him. The environment welcoming him is determined by the degree of spirituality in which he abides. Through death, he reaches that spiritual sojourn that he prepared for himself; he cannot go anywhere else. It's spiritual qualifications that make him gravitate towards those conditions of existence corresponding to his merits and demerits. The great 'law of affinity' governs the process, which results inexorable. Man, after his death, reaches the environment he has prepared for himself: it cannot happen in any other way. He joins those similar to him, gravitates towards those spiritual regions in which he will find himself fully at ease, like in his own environment, like at home. His future abode is already found in his soul, and his spiritual companions are the beings similar to him."

A place of communication with Earth?

By looking at the wealth of communications received from discarnate personalities in the spirit world, it seems reasonable to conclude that these originate from the First Heaven. Here, I am not referring only to the kind of communication we have been looking at in the last few chapters – descriptive, highly structured, clear, "educational" messages aiming to give us an idea of what to expect in the afterlife. I also, and perhaps especially, refer to the countless examples of afterlife communication happening spontaneously (such as in the case of apparitions) and through mediums. Generally, this kind of communication is shorter, less clear, less detailed and essentially focussed on providing bereaved relatives and friends with evidence for survival. Yet, it is of massive value, both for those who receive it and for the scholars of psychical research. Finally, and this is really interesting, I also refer to the many examples of works of art, literature and even science apparently "channelled" from the afterlife.

All of that, I like to believe, comes from the First Heaven. This, after all, is the phase in the afterlife process in which souls are most at ease, following the initial adaptation and before soaring towards more spiritual, much less "Earth-like" dimensions. From this "in-between" plane of existence, reaching back to those living on earth appears to be relatively simpler. Conversely, it has often been pointed out that the higher the sphere, the more difficult it is for spirits to communicate with those on Earth because it becomes increasingly difficult to lower one's vibrations to the Earth vibration as one advances. However, some highly advanced souls, such as Silver Birch and Imperator, both quoted several times in this book, were able to communicate in spite of the difficulties of lowering the vibration level, just as some people in the Earth life seem to be better able to raise their vibrations than others. They said that it was necessary for them to relay messages through other spirits on lower spheres. Moreover, the messages suggest that the more spiritually conscious the medium, the easier it is for spirits from higher realms to communicate through him. William Stainton Moses, the medium for Imperator, and Maurice Barbanell, the medium for Silver Birch, seem to have been highly spiritual during their Earth lives, thus facilitating communication, even if a go-between was required to relay the messages through them.

A spirit called Martha says:

> "We passed quickly through the different stages of our progress, till we arrived at the fifth spiritual sphere [the First Heaven as I call it], which is my present home. I am often with my friends on Earth, and would gladly influence them, and prove my identity to them, if they would render themselves receptive to my power ... When we desire to be with our friends on Earth, we have only to will it, and our desire is instantly gratified. We can visit the spheres below, but not those above us until we are prepared for admission into them by a gradual process of development."

Many from the spirit world have spoken about the communication process and the range of difficulties it is riddled with. For instance, when Rev. Charles Drayton Thomas, a psychical researcher we have mentioned earlier, began sitting with superstar medium of the early

20th century Gladys Osborne Leonard, he quickly made contact with his father, John D. Thomas, and his sister, Etta, receiving much veridical information to prove their identities.

However, he wondered why they had such difficulty in giving their names and the names of others. "It became evident that the giving of a name involved the overcoming of some obstacle, and that usually the difficulty, whatever it might be, was too serious to permit of success," Thomas wrote in his 1928 book, Life Beyond Death. "There is unquestionably a difficulty in transmitting names through trance mediums, though some give them more successfully than do others." With Leonard, the information was usually transmitted by Feda, her spirit control. That is, Leonard would go into a trance and Feda would take over her organism. Feda often spoke of herself in the third person, e.g., "Feda is having difficulty understanding." The discarnate Thomas explained the difficulty to his son:

> "One cannot sometimes get the names right. If I wish to speak about a man named Meadow, I may try that name and find that Meadow is not spoken rightly by Feda. So I then wait and try to insert the idea of a green field, connecting it with the idea of the man described. We always try for a definite thing which will tell you exactly what we mean; but if unable to do that, we have to get as near to it as we can. Sometimes we have to depend upon slender links in giving you the clue."

In a very similar way, after his death, Sir William Barret, a renowned scientist and himself a psychical researcher in life, spoke from the spirit world about the difficulty with communicating names:

> "A detached word, a proper name, has no link with a train of thought except in a detached sense; that is far more difficult than any other feat of memory or association of ideas. If you go to a medium that is new to us, I can make myself known by giving you through that medium an impression of my character and personality,

my work on earth, and so forth. Those can all be suggested by thought impressions, ideas; but if I want to say 'I am Will,' I find that is much more difficult than giving you a long, comprehensive study of my personality. 'I am Will' sounds so simple, but you understand that in this case the word 'Will' becomes a detached word."

By piecing together many different bits of spirit communication, one would have to conclude that, in most cases, the process of communication between the spirit world and people on earth involves not two but four actors. Just like what happens on earth, where people need the help of a gifted medium to be able to communicate across the dimensional barrier, in the spirit world "ordinary" souls need the help of the equivalent of a medium. This "spirit medium" is referred to in the psychical research literature as "control".

Even some superstar human mediums often work under the guidance of their control: he or she helps make contact from the spirit side and drives and coordinates the whole process, often bringing forward different discarnate personalities who will come through in one séance. He or she is generally the first entity to communicate, opening the proceedings, and the last one to come through, bringing the séance to a close. As happens on Earth, however, it appears that certain discarnate personalities have enough "energy", or skills, or a level of development that allows them to come through directly to a medium on Earth and, in certain cases, even directly to their loved ones in the flesh, without the need for either a human medium or spirit control.

Information was also shared about some aspects of what is involved in apparitions and materialisation phenomena. For instance, after dying in the Titanic disaster of 1912, the already quoted William Stead began communicating through various mediums and appearing at some materialisation séances. He explained that there were souls on his side who had the power of sensing people (mediums) who could be used for communication. One such soul helped him find mediums and showed him how to make his presence known.

It was explained to him that he had to visualize himself among the people in the flesh and imagine that he was standing there in the flesh with a strong light thrown upon himself: "I had to hold the visualization very deliberately and in detail, and keep it fixed upon my mind, that at that moment I was there and they were conscious of it." He added that the people at one sitting were able to see only his face because he had visualized only his face: "I imagined the part they would recognize me by." It was in the same way he was able to get a message through: "I stood by the medium, concentrated my mind on a short sentence, and repeated it with much emphasis and deliberation until I could hear part of it spoken through the medium."

A sitter at one of the séances of D. D. Home, one of the most spectacular mediums to ever walk the earth, asked Home's spirit control how spirits make themselves visible, particularly in the case of spontaneous apparitions:

> "At times we make passes (augment the field of energy) over the individual to cause him to see us; sometimes we make the actual resemblance of our former clothing appear exactly as we were known to you on earth. Sometimes we project an image that you see; sometimes you see us as we are with a cloudlike aura of light around us."

Finally, the idea that First Heaven is the level from which most of afterlife communication originates is also supported by the many, extraordinary and very well documented cases in which a perfectly ordinary person on earth, without any previous knowledge or skill, "channels" works of art, literature, music and even scientific information allegedly originating from souls who, as we have been told, continue to tend to their earthly interests in the spirit world.

Possibly the best know case, and the only one we will review here for reasons of brevity, is the one of "Patience Worth". This is the name of the putative author of novels, poems and other writings channeled by Pearl Curran (1883-1937) from 1913 to her death, first through the use of a Ouija board, then by clairvoyant and clairaudient dictation. The material consisted of seven full length novels along with short stories, plays, thousands of poems, and a large number of epigrams and aphorisms. Much of the output was characterized by a pithy, idiosyncratic and archaic language, but was also considered to be of exceptional literary quality. Patience Worth was called a wit, a poet, a dramatist, and a philosopher; some even compared her to Shakespeare, Chaucer, Shelley, and Spenser.

"What is extraordinary about this case is the fluidity, versatility, virtuosity and literary quality of Patience's writings, which are unprecedented in the history of automatic writing by mediums," says Stephen Braude, a Professor Emeritus of philosophy at the University of Maryland Baltimore County and a past president of the American Parapsychological Association.

As one would expect, controversy raged as to whether she really was the spirit of a British-born American who lived in the seventeenth century, as she described herself, or merely a secondary personality formed by Curran's subconscious. Allegations were made that Curran, a St. Louis housewife of limited education plagued by nervous ailments, was a clever trickster. E. H. Garnett, a Chicago lawyer, responded by saying he had known her for years and felt certain that she was not a "falsifier", even though he could offer no reasonable explanation as to her ability:

> "I have on a number of occasions seen her produce, orally and without a moment's hesitation, from twenty to thirty poems on diverse, abstract and concrete subjects given to her by audiences. There is, so far as I know, no other person in the world who can, under such circumstances, even remotely approach this work, either in spontaneity, beauty, perfection of form or in content."

Similar testimonials were given by others, such as the prominent author and publisher Henry Holt:

> "It has of course been suggested that [Pearl Curran] plays the Patience Worth trick for the sake of notoriety,

but how utterly unsupposable it is that a woman capable of composing work of which some specimens are declared by competent critics to be very close to masterpieces, should, loving notoriety, try to throw upon another intelligence the credit of her work, and smother it under a language which nobody uses, and that it requires some effort to understand."

And, Walter Prince, who studied Curran closely for some ten months, and in 1927 published a detailed 509-page analysis of the Patience Worth phenomenon, concluded:

"Either our concept of what we call the subconscious must be radically altered, so as to include potencies of which we hitherto have had no knowledge, or else some cause operating through but not originating in the subconscious of Mrs. Curran must be acknowledged."

Chapter thirteen

Stepping into the Light

As we come closer to what appears as the ultimate destination of souls (please remember that I use the term "soul" without any religious connotation – I use the word interchangeably with words such as "personal consciousness" or "personality", whether in bodily form or discarnate), it is time to take a step back, look at the entire process and draw one very important, I would say fundamental conclusion. I mentioned this conclusion already in the introduction, and I will repeat it here in the form of the key concept for this chapter:

> *In the long term, all this pans out as a project for your own evolution and development. Life, in the material and spiritual worlds, has meaning and purpose.*

Essentially, we have repeatedly and consistently been told that life, at all levels, serves one and only one purpose: learning. In fact – but this is my own, personal reflection, I think that such purpose is even simpler and more fundamental. We exist as individuals, in the material world and in the various spiritual realms, to *have experiences*. Please allow me here a brief metaphysical digression, and then we'll come back to the idea of learning. We will then go on talking about the higher spiritual dimensions which are the subject of this chapter.

The next chapter will introduce the main, overarching, metaphysical conclusion one should draw by comparing the testimony from the three main sources we have been quoting in this book and, critically, by mystics of all human spiritual traditions. We will learn that, across different cultures, languages, epochs, cultural and spiritual traditions, anybody who has had a direct, personal experience of the ultimate nature of reality (which is what the philosophical discipline of metaphysics investigates) has told us that such reality is *one*.

All is one – everything that exists is the emanation, or product, of a single, unique, fundamental reality. This reality is consciousness. Everything, at the end of the day, is consciousness and this consciousness manifests itself in a myriad different ways, in the material universe and in the nonmaterial spheres. Think of a fountain, and of the myriad different forms and combinations the single droplets of water can take – and yet, what appears to us as a changing, mesmerising reality is made up one single substance, water. If you are religiously inclined, you will call this ultimate, essentially, fundamentally conscious reality God. If you are not, you may refer to this as "cosmic consciousness", or "the source" – the substance doesn't change.

This cosmic consciousness, fundamental awareness, by its own nature needs to be conscious of, or aware of, *something*. And so, spontaneously, organically, it originates differentiations within itself, and these differentiations, or features, are individually conscious, at various levels, and all contribute to the ultimate goal of continuing to *produce experiences*. Another water-based representation is that of whirlpools. Think of a stream of water that, under certain conditions, will spontaneously, organically generate a whirlpool. That appears to an observer as a differentiation, a feature of water, but it is and remains water, which temporarily manifests as a whirlpool. So, we embodied humans are whirlpools – temporary manifestations of a "water" which is the fundamental cosmic consciousness. And so are the discarnate humans who evolve in the various levels of the spirit world. We all exist to have experiences and to contribute to the infinite, and yet ever-expanding ocean of experience and consciousness.

In this respect, and this is very, very important, *there is no fundamental difference between the material and nonmaterial worlds*. It is just a matter of levels, dimensions, external appearance – at all levels, as I just said, we exist to have experiences.

After his death, Sir Oliver Lodge, Cambridge academic and among the founders of the Society for Psychical Research, emphatically declared:

> "We have split up life in two parts far too drastically. We have drawn a line, and we must gradually erase the line. We have talked about the spiritual life, and the earth life or the physical life. The two are one and we must make them one again. There is no line, there is no line at all. Man has drawn a line and it must be erased., and it will take some time to erase it completely, but we must work towards that. ... It is only one world. There is only one world and we must take down these ... barriers of illusion that compelled us to think there must be two, because through our limitations and ignorance we are unable to look over the self-erected barrier, or to look through it. It must come down. It is your work, it is our work."

A natural, inevitable soaring

Now, from a human perspective, we also have to understand that material life – the life we live on Earth – is as important, in terms of experiences, as the life we live in the afterlife. Each level provides a kind of experience specific to that level, experiences that could not be had in any other level. *All* of these are very important, and they all contribute to our growth and development. This message comes through quite clearly from what we must assume to be the most advanced spirit communicators. They tell us that it is all about expanding consciousness, thereby progressing to higher and higher levels of vibration referred to as spheres.

We have already cited Rev. Stanton Moses, who channelled an advanced spirit calling himself Imperator. It is very interesting to note that, being a priest of the Anglican Church, Moses found it difficult to accept some of the things Imperator told him as they seemingly conflicted with what he had been taught. This, we believe, is a further argument supporting that the entity Imperator was not simply a creation of Moses' fantasy. Concerning the expansion of consciousness and the development of souls, Imperator said:

> "The true attitude of the spirit is one of striving earnestly in the hope of reaching a higher position than that which it has attained. In perpetually progressing it finds its happiness. There is no finality; none, none, none."

And, the entity known as Silver Birch, communicating through Maurice Barbanell, said:

> "The whole object of earthly life is to have a variety of experiences that will fit the spirit for the next stage beyond earth, when you have to pass into our world. Progress can be quickened by earthly experiences. You must be sharpened, purged, refined. You must experience the heights and the depths. You must have the variety of experiences that earth provides for you.
>
> As awareness increases, the individual realises that he or she possess infinite possibilities, that the road to perfection is an endless one."

Therefore, the inevitable destiny of souls is to continually soar towards higher, more refined states of consciousness, at the same time more profound and more rarefied, from the darkness of matter towards the pure light of consciousness. Like from the bottom of the sea a bubble of air naturally soars towards the surface, growing and expanding as it does so until it merges and dissolves into air, the soul soars, grows and expands until it ultimately merges again with the cosmic consciousness that originally generated it. This grand scheme, this glorious project develops, we are told, over many "cycles", involving repeated sojourns in the earthly and in the spiritual planes. We will talk about this in the chapter about reincarnation.

Therefore, moving from the First Heaven to the spiritual realms is a natural, inevitable process that souls undergo by their own will. At some stage, despite the most beautiful surroundings and the most interesting activities, souls begin to lose interest. They feel, we are told, a natural attraction towards more light, more luminosity, more warmth, more universal, unconditional love, which corresponds to higher planes, more refinement, more advancement.

A world of pure light

Not unexpectedly, available accounts of these higher, ultimately nonmaterial dimensions are brief, and not very many. Very interestingly, unlike testimony about the First Heaven, which comes mostly from spirit communicators, glimpses about the spiritual realms come mostly from NDErs. This presumably owes to the difficulty of conveying the experience of life there in terms of what we can understand and to the practical barriers to communication between such distant and fundamentally different planes of existence. What is clear is that these higher dimensions primarily, and I would say exclusively, belong to inward levels of being.

The posthumous F. W. H. Myers so attempts to describe the higher spiritual realms:

> "...on this level of consciousness pure reason reigns supreme. Emotion and passion, as known by man, are absent. ... Such equanimity becomes the possession of the souls in this last rich kingdom of experience ... they are capable of living now without form, of existing as white light, as the pure thought of their Creator."

Another account from a spirit communicator says:

> "The upper reaches of Heaven, you see, are quite formless, and the houses, gardens, personalities, and cultures that we so carefully cultivate on our way up, as it were, must be ruthlessly cast aside in order to participate in the new ballgame of pure mind. Mind without form, mind eternal and unending.
>
> Our 'higher selves', that eternal identity that has been pulling us slowly through the planes, is essentially a formless, genderless accumulation of light energy, which can, at the slightest flicker of will, be anything and go anywhere."

More details are provided by the experience of one NDEr:

> "The mist started being infiltrated with enormous light and the light just got brighter and brighter and brighter and, it's so bright but it doesn't hurt your eyes, but it's brighter than anything you've ever experienced in your life ... And this enormously bright light seemed almost to cradle me. I just seemed to exist in it and be nurtured by it and the feeling just became more and more and more ecstatic and glorious and perfect."

Another one says:

> "Upon entering the light ... the atmosphere, the energy, it's total pure energy, it's total knowledge, it's total love – everything about it is definitely the afterlife, if you will... As a result of that [experience] I have very little apprehension about dying my natural death ... because if death is anything, anything at all like what I experienced, it's gotta be the most wonderful thing to look forward to, absolutely the most wonderful thing."

One of the most striking and moving NDE testimonies about the higher realms comes from Howard Storm, an atheistic art professor before his NDE who later became a minister of God. In his correspondence to Professor Kenneth Ring, Storm says:

"It was loving me with overwhelming power. After what I had been through, to be completely known, accepted and intensely loved by this being of light surpassed anything I had known or could have imagined. I began to cry, and tears kept coming and coming.

I rose upward, enveloped in that luminous being. Gradually at first, and then like a rocket travelling at great speed, we shot out of that dark and detestable place. I sensed that we traversed an enormous distance, although very little time seemed to elapse. Then, off in the distance, I saw a vast area of illumination that looked like a galaxy. In the centre, there was an enormously bright concentration. Outside the centre, countless millions of spheres of light were flying about, entering and leaving what was a great Beingness at the centre.

The radiance emanating from the luminous spheres contained exquisite colours of a range and intensity that far exceeded anything I as an artist had ever experienced. It was similar to looking at the opalescence one experiences looking into a white pearl or the brilliance of a diamond. As we approached the great luminous centre I was permeated with palpable radiation, which I experienced as intense feelings and thoughts.

And there was a period of time, during my presence in the great light, when I was beyond any thoughts. It is not possible to articulate the exchange that occurred. Simply stated, I knew God loved me."

And yet, somehow, we remain ourselves ...

If I were to summarise what we have learnt so far, I would say that progress consists of progressively shedding imperfections, and striving, and growing toward perfection at all times, at all levels in our adventure. Finally, reaching the highest sphere is sometimes referred to as "merging with the whole" or achieving "Oneness" with the creator - call it God or cosmic consciousness. This final step only happens after several "grand cycles", including accumulating more and more experience at all steps of the process, in the material world and in the nonmaterial spheres. We will explore the concept on oneness in the next chapter and, finally, we will look at reincarnation in the following one.

The idea of merging into the common source of all being, of going back to being what we were all along, may be not particularly appealing to some people as it suggests that we give up our individuality. These people should not worry - Silver Birch, among others, said that such is not the case. "The ultimate is not the attainment of Nirvana," he communicated. "All spiritual progress is toward increasing individuality. You do not become less of an individual. You become more of an individual. You develop latent gifts, you acquire greater knowledge, your character becomes stronger, more of the divine is exhibited through you ... You do not lose yourself. What you succeed in doing is finding yourself."

Philip Gilbert, a sailor killed during World War II, communicated extensively with his mother, Alice Gilbert, by means of automatic writing. On the subject of the possible loss of individuality, he says:

> "The more I learn and merge into my true self, the more difficult it is to express what I see and do. The only absolute certainty is that I, the central I, is unchanged and somewhat as you knew me, only more so. But my form dissolves and reforms itself at will now, for I can think myself into any semblance I please, to do my work."

Frederic Myers communicated much the same message:

> "The merging with the Idea, with the Great Source of spirit, does not imply annihilation. You still exist as an individual. You are as a wave in the sea; and you at last entered into Reality and cast from you all illusions of

appearances. But some intangible essence has been added to your spirit through its long habitation of matter, of ether the ancestor of matter, of what the scientists call empty space, though, if they but knew it, empty space is peopled with forms of an infinite fineness and variety."

Chapter fourteen

Oneness, the final destination

With this, shorter, chapter we are going to take a big leap into the "future" of a soul, although, as we have already seen, speaking of time in human terms when dealing with the spirit world is a mistake. By "leap into the future" I mean that for the moment we will not take into account the empirical evidence about reincarnation, which we'll briefly review in the next chapter, and what we have been told concerning the need to complete a large, possibly very large, number of "lives" in the material world and in the spiritual planes. Instead, we will point at what appears to be the ultimate destiny of all sentient beings – merging back into that cosmic consciousness which generated us in the first place.

In oversimplified terms, we are made to understand that, after sojourning in the higher spiritual planes we talked about in the last chapter, souls essentially go back to an earthly incarnation, typically at a "higher" level than the previous one. The idea of a higher level has often been misunderstood and misinterpreted as coinciding with better material conditions, greater comfort, greater happiness, thereby producing a childish concept of "karma" that sees subsequent incarnations as reward or punishment for the deeds of one's life.

According to the testimony received from our trusted sources, this is obviously not the case: "higher level" refers to the refinement, the level of awareness and understanding, one could say the level of "sophistication" or spiritual maturity of the embodied soul. "Older", wiser, more profound and sophisticated souls rarely live in special material abundance. Rather, in their advanced earthly incarnations, these souls typically devote themselves to helping others in a wide variety of ways, ranging from material assistance to spiritual guidance.

The tell-tale sign of an advanced soul is compassion for other sentient beings, and not a collection of big cars and a villa with swimming pool. These advanced souls are nearer to the completion of the unimaginably vast "grand scheme" of existence – they are nearer to the point at which sojourn in the higher spiritual planes will not be followed by another incarnation, but by the final step into the Light.

Such a final step, as we have already said, simply means shedding any imperfection, getting rid of any leftover illusion or misunderstanding about our essential nature, and going back to fully being what we have always been. This profound concept about the ultimate nature of ourselves and of all what we perceive as reality is at the core of all great spiritual traditions of humanity.

The renowned historian of religions Soares de Azevedo explains how, according to the *perennialist philosophy,* of which I am an ardent supporter, the universal truth is the same within each of the world's orthodox religious traditions, and is the foundation of their religious knowledge and doctrine. Each world religion is an interpretation of this universal truth, adapted to cater for the psychological, intellectual, and social needs of a given culture of a given period of history. This perennial truth has been rediscovered in each epoch by mystics of all kinds who have revived already existing religions, when they had fallen into empty platitudes and hollow ceremonialism

During my more than 20 years of scholarly research, it has been thrilling and utterly fascinating to discover that the testimony we receive from Near-Death Experiencers and spirit communicators on the ultimate nature of reality is absolutely identical to what the mystics of all great spiritual traditions have been telling us for the last thirty centuries. I will then capture this absolute truth with this chapter's key concept:

All is one.

To try to elucidate this, let me start by referring to the few words reportedly uttered by the Buddha himself, emerging from the altered state in which he attained enlightenment. In describing the ultimate nature of reality, and his experience of it, the Buddha simply said:

> Profound calm, free of complexity.
>
> Uncompounded luminosity.

You have to focus on the first line first, and in particular on the words free of complexity, which encapsulate much of the ultimate truth. To give you a little push, I'll suggest a very simple image, one that helped me greatly in my early days, and then we will bring in the quotes from a variety of people. Think of looking at a stormy sea: gigantic waves, each with its own distinctive shape, each moving in a different and complicated matter. Waves crashing on the rocks, dissolving into clouds of droplets, and apparently ceasing to exist. Quite a fitting description of complexity, I believe.

Now, think for a moment – what are the waves? The waves are the sea. The waves are just temporary, superficial manifestations of an underlying, more fundamental reality: the sea. When they crash and apparently dissolve, they simply go back to being what they always had been: the sea. A few meters below the surface of what appears to us as the worst storm, there is profound calm, free of complexity. Stay with this image for a moment, if you can.

So, if I were to express the ultimate truth with my own words, I would say that the mesmerising variety of objects that populate the world – grains of sand, rocks, mountains, planets, stars and, obviously, people – are in fact just temporary, superficial manifestations on a single underlying reality. Do you remember what we said previously about a fountain, or whirlpools in water? These are metaphors illustrating exactly the same concept: appearances – the ever-changing fountain, whirlpool and ocean waves – and reality – the unchanging, single, undifferentiated water. How many times have we heard these concepts already? The Buddhist says that we live in Samsara, the world of illusion: we take the material world that we perceive with our senses as reality, whilst it is not. The Hindu speaks of the veil of Maya, a screen that hides from us the real nature of the world.

What I found totally fascinating is that this age-old wisdom about the ultimate nature of reality, expressed across the centuries by mystics of all spiritual tradition with very similar words, resonates almost identically with what we are told by NDErs and spirit communicators. The bottom line seems to be that anybody who has been able to experience such ultimate reality (either through a spiritual peak experience, a near-death experience or direct experience in the higher spheres of the spirit world) tells us that that the world of creation "emerges" from an underlying reality of a superior order (a "creator", generally referred to as God) just as waves emerge from the sea. Incidentally – but this is a subject that we cannot get into now – this is also precisely what the modern physics is telling us: reality is not the waves, distinct from one another. Reality is the sea, undifferentiated, free of complexity. The creator and the creatures are one. One NDEr so describes this wonderful truth:

> "It became clear to me that all the higher selves are connected as one being, all humans are connected as one being, we are actually the same being, different aspect of the same being."

And see what a spirit communicator has to say:

> "He is the One that appears as many, but is not appearance, because He is what He is. He is infinite because He is the One, eternal because He is unchangeable, in reality indivisible because in reality He is the only one to exist. He is complete, because He is the Totality that includes everything."

And another, who proclaims:

> "I am a manifestation of the universal force that moulds and brings everything into life."

Instead of providing additional quotes from the trusted sources we have been referring to so far, let me bring in a new category of witnesses – the mystics. Mystical experiences are mysterious as they are fascinating. They occur in very different people and in very different circumstances. For some, they just erupt and completely take over consciousness during absolutely normal, day to day life. These moments of sublime, exalted consciousness may last a few minutes or a few hours, but people who experienced them are changed forever. I have a friend, a mountain guide by profession, who had one such experience, and I can tell he certainly is a changed man. For others, mystical experiences may happen during meditation, when contemplating nature, or as a result of a disease or brain impairment. Finally, for some, mystical visions are the product of a lifetime of prayer and contemplation. Regardless of the circumstances that bring about the experience, *everybody essentially says the same thing:* the whole of the experience is "ineffable" – it cannot be properly communicated using human language, but the core, the essence of it is a sense of total unity and communion with everything else. From the early Vedic period in India, 30 centuries before the Christian era, to contemporary NDErs, everybody has been saying the same thing: *all is one, and I am part of that one.* To conclude, let's then look at some of this extraordinary testimony from mystics of the great spiritual traditions of mankind.

For instance, when the Verse of the Throne says "Allah! There no god but he" it doesn't say, as it is superficially believed, that there are no other gods, it proclaims that the ultimate reality is one - Allah is *all there is*.

Similarly, the Jewish Zohar tells us that,

> "if one contemplates things in mystical meditation, everything is revealed as one",

and the Christian idealist Dionysius writes,

> "It is at once in, around and above the world, super-celestial, super-essential, a sun, a star, fire, water, spirit, dew, cloud, stone, rock, all there is".

Meister Eckhart, the thirteen century Dominican monk, wrote:

> "In this breaking-through I receive that I and God are one. Then I am what I was, and then I neither diminish nor increase, for I am then an immovable cause that moves all things".

From the tenth century Sufi mystic Mansur al-Halaj comes the pronouncement,

> "I am the Truth!"

and from eighth-century India, Hindu mystic Shankara inspires us by saying:

> "I am reality without beginning, without equal. I have no part in the illusion of 'I' and 'you', of 'this' and 'that'. I am Brahman, one without a second, bliss without end, the eternal unchanging truth."

And finally, perhaps the most inspiring of the mystics' quotes, the one I found the most beautiful in literary terms and always makes my eyes water, comes from Moses de León, a Jewish Kabbalist and probably the author of the Zohar:

> "God, when he has just decided to launch upon his work of creation is called he. God in the complete unfolding of his Being, Bliss and Love, in which he becomes capable of being perceived by the reason of the heart, is called you. But God, in his supreme manifestation, where the fullness of His Being finds its final expression in the last and all-embracing of his attributes, is called I".

Chapter fifteen

Reincarnation

So, what can we try to conclude from everything we've seen so far in this book? That life extends in time (if we want to use our, human concept of time) and across dimensions, or levels, of which earthly life is the "lower", most physical, most material, "of lowest vibration" as it has often been described. We also have to conclude, as it has been explicitly told to us from our sources, that life is cyclical and has an ascending motion. By "ascending" I mean movement towards more knowledge, more wisdom, more refinement, and by "cyclical" I mean that souls, or personalities, go back and forth between earthly incarnations and sojourns in the spiritual realms many, many times, constantly accumulating experience, knowledge and wisdom. Finally, a point is reached, we are told, at which refinement is such that we can definitively merge back into the "ocean" of cosmic consciousness out of which we appear as individual "waves". If we are to accept this view of the grand scheme of life, then we obviously have to accept the idea of reincarnation.

As far as I am concerned, and to the best of my intellectual honesty, reincarnation is an established fact. The quantity and quality of the evidence, and the depth to which it has been investigated by incredibly credentialed researchers, leave very little doubt that significant aspects of the personality of a deceased person can somehow "reappear" alongside the developing personality of a child born at a later time in another place. At the same time, equally vast but perhaps – in my opinion – less strong evidence exists for the fact that practically anybody, when hypnotically regressed, can vividly remember details of one or more previous lives. All that is further, strong indication of the fact that mind can exist independently of a physical body and that, as we have been saying since the beginning, human personality survives bodily death.

I must admit, however, that reincarnation represents a bit of a challenge for my effort to present the continuum of life in the material and spiritual worlds as a coherent, consistent and – especially – understandable whole. The timing, the place in the sequence of events, the modalities with which a soul returns to a physical body have been explained in rather minute details, but these descriptions come from sources which I personally find less reliable that the three major categories of witnesses we have referred to so far. Most of the information we have about the process comes in fact from people who have been hypnotically regressed to the time before they were born and who offer information about the period in-between earthly incarnations. This information is massive, and, as I said, often quite detailed. It also is, I must say, quite consistent across different witnesses – people who are regressed tend to say rather precisely the same things. This in itself is interesting and encouraging, but I cannot shrug off my doubts deriving from the issue of *false memories*, which research shows can indeed arise during the hypnosis process.

In this chapter, I will therefore limit myself to summarising the evidence we have for reincarnation, for it is an essential element of the grand scheme of life we have been describing so far, and for it is, as I said, an established fact. I will leave it to the reader, if interested, to explore the intricate subject of the actual process of return to the material world through the many sources I quote in the annotated bibliography in annex A.

Conscious past-life memories in children

Perhaps the strongest and best documented evidence in support of reincarnation comes from the extensive, painstaking and extremely detailed work carried out by a number of top researchers of thousands of cases in which a child appears to spontaneously recall memories of a previous life.

The true pioneer of this area of study was Prof Ian Stevenson, an academic psychiatrist of impeccable credentials who, among other things, created and headed for many years the Division of Perceptual Studies at the University of Virginia. Beginning in the late 1950s, Prof Stevenson collected thousands of cases of children who were allegedly able to recall having lived past lives, including names, dates, events and even details about the places where they believed they previously lived. The rigorous, scholarly work carried out for forty years by Ian Stevenson inspired a cohort of equally qualified researchers, notably including his successor at the Division of Perceptual Studies, Dr Jim Tucker, and Prof Erlendur Haraldsson of the University of Iceland.

The subjects in these cases tend to be young children. They typically begin describing a previous life when they are two or three years old, and they usually stop by the age of six to seven. They make the statements spontaneously without the use of hypnotic regression. They describe recent lives, with the median interval between the death of the previous individual and the birth of the child being only 16 months. They also describe ordinary lives, usually in the same country. The one part of the life that is often out of the ordinary is the mode of death, as 70% of the deaths are by unnatural means. Some subjects report having been deceased family members, whereas others say they were strangers in another location. If they give enough details, such as the name of that location, then people have often gone there and identified a deceased individual, the previous personality, whose life appears to match the statements the child made.

Over 2,500 cases have been investigated worldwide. They are easiest to find in cultures with a belief in reincarnation, and the places that have produced the most cases include India, Sri Lanka, Turkey, Lebanon, Thailand, and Burma (Myanmar). However, cases have been found wherever anyone has looked for them, including all continents except Antarctica. Stevenson published a book of European cases, and numerous cases have been found in the United

States as well, some quite striking. In general, cases in the West seem to be less common, but according to experts this is almost certainly due to the fact that parents are reluctant to disclose, even to close friends and family at times, what their children have said.

When cases are investigated, history is obtained from as many people as possible. This includes the subjects, if the children are willing and able to tell investigators about the purported memories, as well as their parents and others who have heard the children describing past-life memories. The other side of the case is then investigated; the previous family is interviewed to determine how accurate the child's statements are for the life of the previous personality. Attempts are made to obtain autopsies or medical records of the previous personality if they are relevant. If the two families have not yet met, tests can also be conducted to see if the subject can recognize people from the previous life.

The average age when subjects begin reporting a past life is 35 months. Some make their statements with detachment, but many show strong emotional involvement in their claims. Some cry and beg to be taken to what they say is their previous family. Others show intense anger, particularly toward killers in cases in which the previous personality was murdered. In general, the stronger the evidence for a connection to the previous life, the more emotion the child shows when talking about that life. Even when the children do show strong emotion, many of them show great intensity one moment, followed by ordinary play a few minutes later. Many seem to need to be in a certain frame of mind to access the memories, and although some are able to recall them on demand, others are not.

The subjects usually stop making their past-life statements by the age of six to seven, and most seem to lose the purported memories. This is the age when children start school and begin having more experiences in the current life, as well as when they tend to lose their early childhood memories. The purported past-life memories often last longer in cases in which the previous personality has been identified, as contact between the two families appears to keep them going longer.

An example of a case with prominent statements is one Stevenson studied in India, that of Kumkum Verma. She lived in a village, but when she was 3.5 years old, she began saying that she had lived in Darbhanga, a city of 200,000 people that was 25 miles away. She named the district of the city where she said she had lived. It was one of artisans and craftsmen, and her family did not know anyone from there. An aunt recorded a number of her statements before anyone attempted to verify them, and though some of her notes were lost, Stevenson was able to get a copy of 18 statements that Kumkum had made. They included her son's name in the life she was describing and the fact that he worked with a hammer, her grandson's name, the town where her father had lived, and personal details such as having an iron safe at home, a sword hanging near the cot where she slept, and a pet snake to which she fed milk.

An employee of a friend of Kumkum's father was from the district in Darbhanga that Kumkum had named, and he went there to search for the previous personality. He found that a woman had died five years before Kumkum was born and whose life matched all of the details listed above. Kumkum's father, a landowner and homeopathic physician, visited the family in Darbhanga once but never allowed Kumkum to go, apparently in part because he was not proud that his daughter seemed to remember the life of a blacksmith's wife.

Many subjects display behaviours that appear connected to the lives they describe. Some show emotions toward various members of the previous family that are appropriate for the relationships that the previous personality had with them, so the children may be deferential toward the previous parents or husband but bossy toward younger siblings of the previous personality, even though they are much older than the subject. These emotions usually dissipate as the children grow older, but there are exceptions. In at least one case, Maung Aye Kyaw of Burma, the child grew up to marry the widow of the previous personality.

Another common behavioural feature is a phobia toward the mode of death of the previous personality. Over 35% of subjects show such phobias in cases involving deaths by unnatural means. These are particularly prevalent in drowning cases, with 31 of 53 showing a fear of being in water. Some subjects display likes and dislikes that are similar to those of the previous personality. For example, Stevenson and Keil studied cases of Burmese children who claimed they were Japanese soldiers killed in Burma during World War II, and some of them complained about the spicy Burmese food and asked for raw fish instead.

Some subjects also show an unfortunate interest in addictive substances such as alcohol and tobacco if the previous personality consumed them. Children often engage in play that appears connected to their past-life reports, particularly play that involves the occupation of the previous personality. Tragically, occasionally children also re-enact the death scene of the previous personality, appearing to show posttraumatic play. To give you an idea of what these cases may look like, let's look at one the best known and most investigated cases in the US, as reported by the Psi Encyclopaedia maintained by the Society for Psychical Research. Please, read this extraordinary story with attention.

The fighter pilot boy

James was born on April 10, 1998 to Bruce and Andrea Leininger while they were living in the San Francisco Bay area. When James was 22 months old, as reported by the parents, his father took him to the James Cavanaugh Flight Museum in Dallas. There he was transfixed by the sight of the WWII planes, and at the end of the visit had to be forced to leave. Passing a toy shop when James was just shy of two years, his mother noticed a display bin filled with plastic toys and boats: she pulled out a little propeller plane and handed it to James, adding, "Look there's even a bomb underneath it." He said, "That's not a bomb, Mummy. That's a *dwop* tank." Talking about this with her husband later she learned that a drop tank is an extra fuel tank fitted to an aircraft to extend its range.

Shortly after turning two, James began having nightmares, as often as five times a week, in which he would scream and kick his legs in the air, crying "Airplane crash! Plane on fire! Little man can't get out!"

At 28 months, in response to questions, he told his parents the little man was himself and that his plane had been shot by the Japanese. Asked how did he know they were Japanese, he answered , "Because of the red sun". About two weeks later, he added more details: his name had been James; he'd flown a Corsair; and he'd flown from a "boat", whose name he gave as *Natoma* – which despite sounding Japanese he insisted was American. Over the next three months, James added that he'd had a friend, a fellow pilot named Jack Larsen, and that he'd been shot down near Iwo Jima.

In play, James crashed his toy planes into furniture, breaking off the propellers. He also began expressing his memories in art, obsessively drawing naval-aerial battles between Americans and Japanese, in which planes were burning and crashing, bullets and bombs exploding all around. These were always WWII scenes, with propeller-driven aircraft, not jets or missiles. He named the American aircraft as Wildcats and Corsairs, and referred to Japanese planes as 'Zekes' and 'Bettys', explaining that the boy's name referred to fighter planes and the girl's name to bombers (this was correct). He sometimes signed the drawings "James 3", and when asked why, said he was "the third James", (possibly a reference to him following James Huston Jr.). When buckling himself into the back of the car he would often mime putting on headgear, a movement that his mother recognized during a visit to a local airshow, when he mounted the cockpit of a Piper Cub and put on the pilot's headgear.

Bruce Leininger was uncomfortable with the idea of reincarnation and began to research his son's statements in the firm hope of ruling this out. He was already aware that the Corsair was an American WWII-era plane. Searching the Internet, he discovered that the USS Natoma Bay was an aircraft carrier that served in the Pacific in WWII and was part of an Iwo Jima operation, also that a pilot named Jack Larsen had been based on the ship.

He then started to approach Natoma Bay veterans, who proved forthcoming. An initial candidate for James's memories, Jack Larsen, turned out however not to have been killed. Attention then shifted to James McReady Huston, Jr. of Pennsylvania, who'd been killed near Iwo Jima aged 21, and whom James's statements seemed to match. Clinching testimony came from eyewitnesses who'd seen the plane was hit in the engine, which exploded in a ball of fire before it crashed, confirming James's account. A unit logbook recording the crash can now be viewed online.

During a visit to James Huston's surviving sister, Anne Barron, she verified other details James had made earlier about his previous family, including the problems caused by his father's alcoholism. After speaking with James, she became convinced that he was indeed her brother reborn, from his knowledge of facts known only to Huston, such as the existence of a painting by their mother of Anne as a child.

University of Virginia's Prof Jim Tucker wrote an informal account of the case as a chapter in his 2013 book *Return to Life: Extraordinary Cases of Children Who Remember Past Lives*, then published a formal case report in 2016. As part of the investigation, Tucker reviewed the video footage shot by ABC in 2002, crucially *before* James Houston had been identified. The verified statements from the footage were: his plane was shot in the engine and crashed in water; he died in the battle of Iwo Jima; the plane was on fire and sank, and he could not get out; he flew a Corsair; his plane flew off a boat; his plane was shot down by the Japanese; Corsairs tended to get flat tires when they landed.

Tucker argued against the possibility of a complex fraud, citing, amongst other things, the length of time the case took to develop and the large number of people involved in the investigation. He also ruled out fantasy, since James's nightmares and behaviours such as repeatedly crashing toy planes, and drawing in the way he did, are more characteristic of children who have suffered traumas. With regard to coincidence, Tucker considered the possibility of such detailed statements exactly matching the identity and circumstances of a particular deceased individual by pure chance to be infinitesimally small. Finally, Tucker noted that all the documented statements leading to the identification of Huston were made by James himself. He could not have read about Huston or the Natoma Bay. Nor could he have been exposed to any television program on these topics. His parents and the people around him had no knowledge of them.

Birthmarks and birth defects

In addition to the purported memories, a number of the children have had birthmarks or birth defects that appeared to match wounds, usually fatal ones, suffered by the previous personalities. Stevenson published a 2,200-page work that documented over 200 such cases, as well as a shorter synopsis. Examples include a girl, born with markedly malformed fingers, who seemed to remember being a man whose fingers were cut off, and a boy, born with stubs for fingers on his right hand, who seemed to remember the life of a boy in another village who lost the fingers of his right hand in a fodder-chopping machine.

Another example is Chanai Choomalaiwong, a boy from Thailand. When he was three years old, he began saying that he had been a teacher named Bua Kai who had been shot and killed one day as he rode his bicycle to school. He begged to be taken to his parents, that is, Bua Kai's parents, and he named the village where he said they lived. Eventually, he and his grandmother took a bus that stopped in a town near that village. His grandmother reported that after they got off the bus, Chanai led her to a house where an older couple lived. Chanai appeared to recognize the couple, who were the parents of Bua Kai Lawnak, a teacher who had been shot and killed on the way to school five years before Chanai was born.

No autopsy report was available for Bua Kai Lawnak, so Stevenson interviewed witnesses who saw the body. His widow reported that the doctor involved in the case said that her husband had been shot from behind, because the small, round wound on the back of his head was a typical entry wound, whereas the larger, more irregularly shaped wound on his forehead was typical of an exit wound. Chanai was born with two birthmarks, a small, round birthmark on the back of his head, and a larger, more irregularly shaped one toward the front.

Past life regression

Past life regression is a form of guided hypnotherapy that appears to elicit memories relating to previous lives. In a large number of documented cases, subjects have recalled characteristics appropriate to the life they are recalling (when these are known), and the period in which it occurred, in surprising detail, and apparently far beyond their conscious knowledge. In combination, the obscurity of the information, realistic presentation of character and emotional identification on the part of the subject have convinced many people of the reality of reincarnation.

Hypnotic regression came to public notice with a case published in 1956 by a Colorado businessman and hypnotherapist, Morey Bernstein. Bernstein had worked with Virginia Tighe, a subject who proved especially susceptible to a deep trance state, in order to investigate the possibility of regressing a patient beyond birth to previous existences. In her first session, Tighe starting speaking with an Irish accent and gave details of a life in which she was born in 1798 in Cork, named Bridget Kathleen Murphy and married a Belfast barrister. During this and subsequent sessions Tighe provided extraordinarily colourful and intricate details about nineteenth-century Ireland, referring to songs, farming methods, books, coins and furniture of the period. She named two Belfast shops that were later found to have existed, and used terms that were now redundant but had then been current.

Following the publication of the book *The Search for Bridey Murphy*, the popularity of the case phenomenal, and verification of the information provided by Mrs Tighe therefore went to an unprecedented level. Several American newspapers put investigative journalists on the case, and great efforts were deployed in Ireland, including the hiring of a law firm to carry out investigations locally and the involvement of local librarians, literature professors, language experts and various other researchers. On the whole, an astonishing number of details were indeed confirmed.

Inevitably, organised sceptics and a part of the press tried to "debunk" the case. Despite their claims, these efforts ended up not getting very far. After reviewing the case and the attempts to debunk it, Prof Stevenson commented, "What some critics of the case provided were *suppositions* of possible sources of the information about Bridey Murphy, not *evidence* that these had been the sources. It is one thing to speculate on possible sources of information and quite another to show a specific matching between a subject's statements and a definite source of information providing the ingredients of those statements." In his review of the case, Washington University philosophy professor CJ Ducasse concluded that, while it does not prove that Tighe is the reincarnation of Bridey Murphy – since her existence was not confirmed historically – it provides evidence that paranormal knowledge of obscure aspects of nineteenth-century Ireland was given under hypnosis.

From the 1960s, hypnotic regression with the aim of eliciting past life memories gained extraordinary popularity, involving very serious practitioners and researchers, but also quite a number of misguided, deluded individuals, and even some charlatans. Despite the variety of the sources, the amount of evidence produced in the last sixty through this methodology is indeed colossal, and some apparently very convincing.

Another intriguing finding about these apparent memories is that both generalities and details of the previous lives subjects claim to remember appear to accord quite well with social and economic data provided by historians. The work of Helen Wambach, a psychology PhD, is particularly interesting in this respect. Starting in the late 1960s, she employed hypnotic regression techniques with subjects in the state of California, reaching a total of 1088 over a ten-year period. Following sessions, she carried out research to discover how well the details matched the period to which the subject had been regressed, such as clothing, housing, money, common objects and people they knew at the time. The details given during sessions were so abundant that Wambach devised a method of statistical analysis to organize them in a reliable way. To make the data more manageable, she restricted her questions during the sessions to certain types and defined ten time periods over the last four thousand years to which subjects would be regressed.

Wambach considered her subjects' recollections to be impressively accurate, finding only eleven discrepancies out of the 1,088 data sheets collected. She researched details of clothing, footwear, food and utensils that were consistent with specific statements made in the regressions which, moreover, were often described in more detail than historians could provide. She also investigated types of death such as disease, old age or violence. She reported that 50.6% of the past lives reported were male and 49.4% were female, a proportion that corresponds with biological data. Distribution of class was similarly accurate. Most subjects chose periods when the population was known to be high, as would be expected.

Despite all that, however, I personally consider evidence from past life regression less convincing than the one from spontaneous recall by children. First of all, a number of alternative parapsychological explanations have been proposed, including ESP ("mind reading") and exposure to the memories of deceased humans. Secondly, and very importantly, some narratives have been traced to printed sources, suggesting the presence of *cryptomnesia* – unconscious recall of facts in books and films, or of past events, to which the subject has been exposed, however fleetingly and however long ago. Thirdly, there remain serious reservations about the authenticity of memories recovered under hypnosis, especially given the phenomenon of false memory syndrome.

Important conclusion

I apologise for using the qualification "important" again, after having used it for the Introduction chapter of this book. I do this to draw the reader's attention to sections that are often considered unimportant and possibly skimmed over or simply ignored. In the particular case of this book, such sections are indeed "important". You will remember that in the introduction I set out the general scope of this work, its aim and expected – or hoped for – results for the target readership. In this conclusion, I want to try to bring together the essential lessons we have learned from our trusted sources, in the hope they will "etch" themselves onto your heart and soul, and will ease any remaining fear you may have concerning the transition we call death.

To do so, I will go back to the statements I used in the introduction and expand and reinforce them in light of what we have learnt.

Let's then begin by recalling how over 60 years of scientific research into Near-Death Experiences tell us beyond reasonable doubt that prolonged, lucid, organised experiences are had by people whose brain functions are totally compromised, such as during anaesthesia, coma, unconsciousness and, crucially, when clinically dead. In tens of thousands of carefully investigated cases, whilst having no functioning brain NDErs go through a highly complex experience which has many similar elements regardless of context, culture, race, religion, sex, age or socioeconomic condition of the experiencer. Furthermore, whilst having no functioning brain NDErs build rich memories of the experience which are recalled in minute details 20, 25 or 30 years after the events. Finally, this fundamental human experience determines profound, far-reaching and long-lasting psychological and behavioural changes in those who've had it at a time when they had no functioning brain. As a whole range of explanations for the phenomenon have been proposed and failed to account for the evidence, NDEs are labelled as a "medical mystery". However, by looking at the science of Near-Death Experiences, the only conclusion we can draw is that

Your mind, your personality, your consciousness, your memories, all that you identify with yourself, with your feeling of being alive, are not dependent on your functioning physical brain.

It is important to remember that this, in fact, is the position taken by *all* the scientists who have dedicated their lives to the study of the NDE phenomenon, with virtually no exceptions.

What appears to us in the material world as death, therefore, from the point of view of the personal experience is essentially a non-event. If the person is conscious at the moment in which the body stops functioning, there is *no interruption* in the flow of consciousness – the only "signal" that something important has happened is the sudden cessation of discomfort and pain, if they were present leading up to death. If the person is unconscious, the death of the body is experienced as waking up from sleep. As we have said

When your brain dies, your mind and personality will continue to exist. It will still be you, and it will feel exactly like you, only without a physical body.

We have heard from our witnesses that the early moments of life without a physical body may be confusing or disorienting. As consciousness adapts to the new conditions, many retain the experience of some form of physical body, an experience which gradually fades as the soul gradually ascends towards higher spiritual realms. We have been repeatedly told that knowing what to expect, being prepared to the continuation of consciousness, greatly reduces any disorientation or confusion the soul may experience in the early afterlife.

Looking at the grand scheme of existence, as explained to us by spirit communicators and taking into account evidence for reincarnation, it is clear that a soul's "life" extends over a very long period of time – as understood by our earthly standards – and includes a number of cycles consisting of an incarnation in the material world followed by a sojourn in the spirit world. Therefore

You most probably have gone through this transition from the physical to the spiritual world many times already, as this is not likely to be your first incarnation.

So, we have understood that at the moment of the death of the body our consciousness simply continues to do what it does naturally – having experiences. The experiences in the spirit world are very complex and, while some details vary between an individual soul and another, the overall pattern as described by spirit communicators is very consistent:

After the demise of your physical body, you will spend a certain amount of time in the various levels of the spirit world, and then you will probably, but not necessarily, incarnate again.

We have learnt that at the beginning the soul dwells in "lower" spiritual planes and has experiences closer to the ones she had during life in the material world. Part of these experiences is a life review in which every single deed and every single thought of the earthly life are somehow relived and assessed in their consequences. This is no judgement and there is no sentence at the end of it. Rather, this life review is one of the high points in the soul's grandiose voyage of experiencing, learning, growing and refining. We also learned that, past the life review, the discarnate individual naturally, organically ascends to higher, more refined spiritual realms, progressively more distanced from Earth and the experiences of material life. At some stage, however, most souls, not having yet reached full wisdom and development, begin considering another period of experience, education and development in the material world. This is because, we are told, as much as a number of experiences can only be had in the spiritual world, so there are crucial experiences that can only be had in the material reality. Cycle after cycle, the grand scheme of existence looks like and upwards spiral, ever ascending towards more experience, more knowledge, more wisdom – in a word, *greater light*:

In the long term, all this pans out as a project for your own evolution and development. Life, in the material and spiritual worlds, has meaning and purpose.

At their most essential, the meaning and purpose of existence is *having experiences*. Whether incarnate or discarnate, we are *sentient beings*. We are individual waves emerging out of an ocean which is *sentience* itself. We are fragments of the cosmic consciousness, whose ultimate nature is awareness – awareness not as a concept but rather as a verb: the very action of being aware, of knowing, of having experiences. By ascending the spiral of our development as individual souls, we will eventually merge back – or ascend to, if you want – the ocean of cosmic consciousness out of which we have appeared in the first place.

My last words for you are a powerful meditation I conceived towards the end of the darkest months of the ghastly COVID pandemic, an event that has proven to be a "perfect psychological storm" for me, resulting in a severe personal crisis of anxiety and depression. This meditation, progressively refined as I added more elements based on what I learnt in 20 years of scholarly study of psychical research and philosophy of consciousness and on my own spiritual practice, helped me a great deal to emerge from the pits of fear and despair. I repeat these words every day, several times a day. In doing so I see them sinking progressively deeper into my awareness, understanding and consciousness. As they do so, the continuously acquire new and deeper meanings, and I realise that they constituted a major, and most probably *the*, turning point in my crisis.

I humbly and wholeheartedly recommend that you do the same.

Glasgow, 9 March 2021

You have the experience of a body growing old, for it is of a nature of growing old and you cannot escape it.

You have the experience of progressive decay and, possibly, illness, for the body is of a nature of decaying and attracting illness and you cannot escape it.

Although the body is of a nature of dying, and you cannot escape it, you will not have the experience of death. When the body stops functioning, there is no interruption in the flow of consciousness. The only experience that may signal the moment of passing is a cessation of physical discomfort or suffering, if present before the death of the body.

Instead of the experience of a physical body in a material world, you will have the experience of a non-physical body evolving through the lower levels of the spirit world.

As the experience of a non-physical body gradually dissolves, you will have the experience of soaring to and evolving through the higher levels of the spirit world.

You may have the experience of preparing for a new incarnation.

Whether you reincarnate or ascend to the ultimate heights of reality, you will continue having experiences.

Because you are the experiencer.

You are the unchanging Witness with no beginning and no end, unborn, undead throughout lifetimes, for you are of a nature of having experiences.

You are experience itself.

You are Being, Awareness, Bliss.

Appendix A

Sources and essential bibliography

General Parapsychology/Psychic Powers

Parapsychology: A Handbook for the 21st Century edited by Etzel Cardeña,, John Palmer, et al.

The Conscious Universe: the Scientific Truth of Psychic Phenomena by Dean Radin PhD

Parapsychology: The Science of Unusual Experience edited by David Groome and Ron Roberts

The Parapsychology Revolution: A Concise Anthology of Paranormal and Psychical Research edited by Robert Schoch PhD

Beyond the Occult: Twenty Years' Research into the Paranormal by Colin Wilson

The ESP Enigma: The Scientific Case for Psychic Phenomena by Diane Hennacy Powell MD

Extraordinary Knowing: Science, Skepticism and the Inexplicable Powers of the Human Mind by Elizbeth Lloyd Mayer PhD

Near-Death Experiences

The Handbook of Near-Death Experiences: Thirty Years of Investigation edited by Janice Miner Holden, EdD, Bruce Greyson, M.D., & Debbie James, RN/MSN

Life After Life: The Bestselling Original Investigation That Revealed "Near-Death Experiences" by Raymond Moody, M.D.

Consciousness Beyond Life: The Science of the Near-Death Experience by Pim van Lommel, M.D.

Evidence of the Afterlife: The Science of Near-Death Experiences by Jeffrey Long, M.D.

Science and the Near-Death Experience: How Consciousness Survives Death by Chris Carter

Lessons from the Light: What we can learn from the near-death experience by Kenneth Ring, PhD

Return from Death: An Exploration of the Near-Death Experience by Margot Grey

The Purpose of Life as Revealed by Near-Death Experiences from Around the World by David Sunfellow

Wisdom of Near Death Experiences: How Understanding NDEs Can Help Us Live More Fully by Penny Sartori PhD

After: A Doctor Explores What Near-Death Experiences Reveal about Life and Beyond by Bruce Greyson

Near-Death Experiences, The Rest of the Story: What They Teach Us About Living and Dying and Our True Purpose by P.M.H. Atwater

Deathbed visions

Deathbed Visions: How the Dead Speak to the Living by Sir William Fletcher Barrett

At the Hour of Death: A New Look at Evidence for Life After Death, by Erlendur Haraldsson Ph. D. and Karlis Osis Ph. D.

One Last Hug before I Go: The Mystery and Meaning of Deathbed Visions by Carla Wills-Brandon

Visions, Trips and Crowded Rooms: Who and What You See Before You by David Kessler

A Call from Heaven: Personal Accounts of Deathbed Visits, Angelic Visions, and Crossings to the Other Side by Josie Varga

In the Light of Death: Experiences on the threshold between life and death by Ineke Koedam

We'll Meet Again: Irish Deathbed Visions – Who You Meet When You Die by Colm Keane

Glimpses of Eternity: Sharing a Loved One's Passage From This Lifetime to the Next by Raymond Moody and Paul Perry

Afterlife Communication

Is There an Afterlife? A Comprehensive Overview of the Evidence by David Fontana PhD

The Departed Among the Living: An Investigative Study of Afterlife Encounters by Erlendur Haraldsson PhD

The Archives of the Mind by Archie Roy PhD

Talking With the Spirits: Ethnographies Form Between The Worlds edited by Jack Hunter and David Luke

Spirit Communication: A Comprehensive Guide to the Extraordinary World of Mediums, Psychics and the Afterlife by Roy Stemman

Manifesting Spirits: An Anthropological Study of Mediumship and the Paranormal by Jack Hunter PhD

The Medium Explosion: A Guide to Navigating the World of Those Who Claim to Communicate with the Dead by Robert Ginsberg

Afterlife

Life Beyond Death: What Should We Expect? by David Fontana PhD

The Afterlife Revealed: What Happens When We Die by Michael Tymn

Living On: A Study of Altering Consciousness After Death by Paul Beard

Deathbed Visions: the Physical Experiences of the Dying, by Sir William Fletcher Barrett

Journey of Souls: Case Studies of Life Between Lives by Michael Newton PhD

Printed in Great Britain
by Amazon